Confessions of a Wondering Generality

*Living in My Head
to Loving in My Heart*

CHAD WITMEYER

Copyright © 2024
Chad Witmeyer

Performance Publishing
McKinney, TX

All Worldwide Rights Reserved.
All rights reserved. No part of this publication may be reproduced, stored in a retrieval system or transmitted, in any form or by any means, electronic, mechanical, recorded, photocopied, or otherwise, without the prior written permission of the copyright owner, except by a reviewer who may quote brief passages in a review.

ISBN: 978-1-961781-52-8

I dedicate this book to my brother, Kirkpatrick Forrest Witmeyer, who died too soon to read this book and to know that he was much loved and his life could mean so much to so many. I feel that this book was written for him and because of him it was made possible. Thank you, Kirk

"Caution, Reader, you are in for a ride! I've known Chad Witmeyer for 40+ years and know he has a "helpful heart." This is evidenced by his helping me early in my career with the Zig Ziglar Corporation and providing woodworking services for my son's Cub Scout Pinewood Derby races (he and my son finished a strong second!). Throughout those years, I felt Chad holding back on his friends and business associates. In this book, you will discover the causes of this and the path he is taking toward redemption. It's been said that "potential is a heavy burden." Chad bore that burden, and he has now discovered the reason. More importantly, he's discovered the path to move closer to that potential. We all benefit from his candor in sharing how we can reach ours."

Bryan Flanagan,
Founder & CEO Flanagan Training
Learn! Laugh! Grow!
www.flanagantraining.com

"I am nobody famous. I am not an author, celebrity, or even an influencer. I am merely the author's daughter. I never thought my dad would write a book. Well, scratch that. I figured he might start one but never finish. Such was the pattern of his life. He will tell you all about it, just ask him. But if you are reading this, it means you have his book in hand. Don't put it down. What you need to know is that I had lost hope in meeting the man God created my dad to be. He was floundering; wallowing in his head, his past, his insecurities, and his inability to truly turn everything over to Jesus. Sound familiar? His story is almost everyone's story in a lot of ways. If you are looking for guidance, encouragement, and a true testimony, keep reading. If you have lost hope that change can occur at any age, read this book. It is never too late to surrender your life to Jesus and live your purpose in Him."

Katherine Lemons,
Chad Witmeyer's Daughter and Unofficial President of The Nibb's Fan Club
Realtor®, The Lemons Group, Fraser Realty

"Chad Witmeyer is one of the most focused people I know. He is focused on serving others, building friendships, investing in family relationships, and thinking of others above himself. And he does it all out of a singular, white-hot motive: to love the Lord fully and to love his neighbor unselfishly. Chad wasn't this way when I first met him – he was unfocused, dazed, and confused, or, to use his word, distracted. But what a turnaround has occurred in his life! This book gives you a front-row seat to the grace of God active in the life of one man."

Paul Basden,
Senior Pastor, Preston Trail Community Church, Frisco, Texas

"I have known Chad for decades. I have seen the highs and the lows of his life. But I have never seen Jesus in his life as I am seeing Him now! Chad's face literally glows with the love for his Savior! He's different, and it shows!

As Chad admits, he took a lifetime to reach the point where he realized he had to make a deep-down, honest decision to change the direction of his life. He encourages us not to wait and gives us direction on how to do just that! His journey is amazing, full of wisdom, guidance and encouragement. I feel strongly that Chad's book will change your life, and your love for the Lord will deepen to a depth you never knew possible!

"Just go, light the fire, and move toward the light. It's ok."

Cindy Ziglar Oates,
your favorite sister-in-law
Customer Service Whisperer, Zig Ziglar Corp

"I have been working with Chad Witmeyer since 2018. Chad has been on a very honest journey, facing many difficult issues and experiences from his past. This journey has led him to healing, insights, and a life-giving path that he walks now. I have truly been inspired and encouraged by Chad's journey, and believe you will be also when you read this book that holds many powerful insights."

Eric Atherton,
Executive Coach and Facilitator, CEO & Founder, Resolute BC
An Inspiring Story of Redemption and Metamorphosis

"As I think back on that evening in January 2020 when seven of us first met Chad at the kick-off meeting of our "Rooted" group, I'm struck by the power of our Lord to transform in miraculous and wondrous ways. Over the last four years, I've had the opportunity to witness a truly remarkable journey of faith and life change that all started with Chad's decision to "jump off the cliff" and let God take the steering wheel of his life. On these pages, Chad transparently and humbly shares his journey from the depths of despair to a Christ-centered life filled with rich purpose, meaning, fulfillment, true happiness, and a daily commitment to becoming the man God created him to be. Chad's message is simple—it's never too late to "jump off the cliff" and pursue the abundant life God desires for us. His story should inspire us all!"

Gary Dias,
Principal & Managing Consultant, Dias & Associates Strategic Solutions, LLC

"In relating life's lessons, in both humorous and profound ways, Chad checks all the boxes. Men of Distinction is a mentoring initiative for high school young men who need an additional, caring voice in their lives. Chad's involvement as a mentor is like a tall drink of refreshing water. He's real, he's relatable, and he's invaluable as a mentor and equally as a friend."

Jim Mustain,
Pastor, Founder, and Executive Director of Loving Community

"Having had the pleasure of knowing the "before" and "after" Chad Witmeyer, I have the joy of witnessing true, genuine spiritual repentance (and in a man, yet!) and renewal. This is an exciting read. Let his story inspire you to your most meaningful and fulfilling life -- "beyond what you might ask or think!"

Laurie Magers,
Executive Assistant to Zig and Tom Ziglar

Chad bares his soul, sharing a raw and transformative journey from heartbreak to self-discovery. It is a tale of loneliness, redemption, and the divine whisper that shaped his purpose and everything. I am sure this book will be a blessing to anyone in their lows. Thanks, Chad.

Tim Chandran,
VP Strategy and Delivery, Ericsson Inc.

It's never too late. *Confessions of a Wondering Generality* Is a powerful road map for anyone who is ready to get off the highway to pointless and on to the road to purpose. Make today the turning point in your life, and devour this book. Chad shares his story in such a way that it will give you hope and encouragement, no matter where you are on the road of life.

Tom Ziglar,
CEO of Zig Ziglar Corporation

Having a close personal connection with Chad, I can personally vouch for the profound and transformative journey he has embarked on. The book stands as a powerful representation of his tenacity, his profound faith, and his unyielding dedication to uncovering the truth (his and ours). He openly shares his battles with distractions, his quest for purpose, and his ultimate realization of the bountiful life promised by God to all believers through his sincere and frank reflections.

Upon reading, I was deeply moved by Chad's bravery in sharing his personal narrative and his openness to vulnerability with the aim of aiding others. His wisdom on the perils of thresholds and the crucial importance of living life intentionally hold relevance both for the present times and for all times.

I highly recommend this book to anyone on a quest to lead a more meaningful and purpose-driven life. Chad's path serves as a potent reminder that there is always room for change, growth, and the discovery of the abundant life that is in store for all of us through Christ.

Patrick Moore
Director - Global Tech Strategy & Commercialization, Walmart

My brother-in-law, Chad Witmeyer, has truly surprised me with this book. I have known him for almost half a century, and in *Confessions of a Wondering Generality*, I have come to know him as he knows himself. Consequently, I love him far more than ever before. I love his total trust in Jesus, his confidence in his relationship with Jesus, and the love of Jesus he shares with everyone he meets. I pray his candid revelations about himself, and the way his life has turned full face to Christ will impact your life with Jesus in the same positive way. Thank you, Chad, for your encouragement and love.

Julie Ziglar Norman,
your favorite sister-in-law
Author & Realtor®, Ziglar Realty

CONTENTS

Acknowledgements.................................xv

Introduction.....................................xix

Chapter 1: Why Did I Write This Book and Why Should You Care? 1

Chapter 2: Hypocrisy: Managing Image or Forming Character 11

Chapter 3: Life Gets in the Way 21

Chapter 4: You Can't Delegate Your Faith or Prayers ..31

Chapter 5: Rewiring a Brain 43

Chapter 6: Distractions Can Kill 53

Chapter 7: The Culture War Distraction 71

Chapter 8: What Do You Have to Lose? 85

Chapter 9: The Prime Directive 101

Chapter 10: The Promise of The Abundant Life.......119

Chapter 11: K.I.S.S..............................135

Chapter 12: What's the Point of It All and Why You? ..149

Conclusion 161

Acknowledgements

Dr. Paul Brand and Phillip Yancy, in their book, *In His Image*, liken the incredible human body to the church founded by Jesus Christ, Jesus being the head and all believers the body. Each member of the body is essential to every other member and to Jesus as the head. Everyone I have encountered in my life has had an impact on me, whether I knew it at the time or not. Without the influence of each person, knowingly or unknowingly to them, I would not be, and could not be the person I am today. God placed everyone in my life purposefully, intended for my benefit. Therefore, I owe far too many more people than I can credit here. Thank you all!

Gladstone Oliver Thompson: Known to his friends as "G.O.," He probably began my journey to finding Jesus before I knew I was searching. I hired him to work with me in the endeavor that brought me to Dallas, Texas. He was a master craftsman who taught me volumes about repairing and building furniture, and so much more about life. He was an Assemblies of God preacher from Jamaica and would at some time every day break into loud song praising God, and I, as the only audience, loved it.

Eric Atherton: My friend and Biblical counselor for over four years, weekly for three years and continuing to this day twice a month. He is hugely responsible for taking a totally devastated man from his collision with a spiritual and emotional brick wall in life to a completely (well, almost) rewired and rejuvenated man of restored faith, belief, and love with a well-defined purpose and mission. And Eric also gave me what became my morning start-up prayer.

Dr. Rick Housewright: A friend, gifted chiropractor, as well as a true disciple of Christ. Sessions with Rick were as much a time of spiritual adjustment as they were a physical realignment.

Laurie Magers: Friend and co-worker, I have known Laurie for over forty five years and love and respect her. Laurie was my editor for this book and her advice and opinions were invaluable.

Thomas Ann Hines: My friend and long-time customer who gifted me with an almost new pc, which I have used to write much of this book.

Katherine Lemons: My incredible daughter who believed in me despite my failures and poor decisions. She is a fantastic mother and wife, in addition to being a great friend and role model to many.

Jonathan McGehee: The psychologist who helped me begin my journey to wholeness after crashing and burning.

Eight men of faith: My brothers in Christ, who allowed me into their lives without judgment, with plenty of love and support, contributing in a huge, immeasurable way to my re-birth, like a butterfly, into a man of unlimited possibilities and purpose.

Paul Basden: My friend, pastor, and fellow beggar who has encouraged me to be genuine, transparent, and open to all the blessings that God has in store for me.

Jim Mustain: My friend who encouraged me to volunteer my time and experience to help others.

The Preston Trail Community Church family, whom I love dearly, and the individuals who helped in so many, many ways to save this lost soul, leading me to see the abundant life that awaits us all.

Michelle Prince: A dear and long-time friend, a sister in Christ, who reminded me of the value of the uniqueness of my life's experience, encouraged me to share my story in this book, and walked alongside me through the process of making it happen.

Roger and Chris Bohm: Cousins I grew up with, with whom I survived death-defying experiences, supported me during times when I needed it most, always loving me for who I was and whom I love very much.

Pam and Chris Mauldin: The friends who worked for months to persuade me to finally accept a blind date with Suzan Ziglar, who also was very resistant to the idea. Suzan became my wife of 17 years before she went home to be with Jesus.

Zig Ziglar: I can't say enough about this incredible man who influenced the lives of so many people in the world to become better and love others, yet did not neglect to love and believe in his own family. He often said that love is spelled t.i.m.e. He invested the time and demonstrated love to each one of us in his family, and I regret that I am only now realizing how huge his contribution to my life has been, to this day and long after he went home to be with Jesus.

Jean and John Stinebaugh: My two very dear friends who walked beside me during good and bad times and remain to this day examples of how to love our neighbors. I consider John to be my best friend, even though we have been out of touch for too long.

Todd Duncan: A friend and business associate who hired me and then fired me. I owe Todd much for hiring me to do a job that I should have been able to do well, but my performance was disappointing and it was absolutely the right decision to fire me.

INTRODUCTION

What's the <u>Point</u>?
What is the Purpose of Life?
Why Am I Here? Why Are <u>You</u> Here?

When I started writing this book I was 73, and it was slightly more than two years after my wife of twenty years had announced we would sell our home and separate, the marriage over. Her main reasons were we had no relationship with each other left, and I was "living in my head." The second was I had devolved into viewing pornography and that equated with infidelity. I would equate it now to running into a brick wall at full speed (without safety gear, I might add).

On May 10, 2019, the sale of the house closed and I moved into an apartment, alone, and she moved into her own apartment, alone. I found myself sitting in the dark, looking around a 630 square foot, one room apartment, and I realized I was really and completely, really alone (I know, I said that twice). If the first heart-stopping moment was when I was told we were separating, the second sudden heart-stopping moment occurred then. Alone, in that apartment, alone (there, I said it again but I was really alone), I felt the impact of a proverbial 2x4 to the forehead, like someone stepped back and took a full swing. That was when the totality of the moment finally sank in. Life had really and suddenly changed, taken a left turn, and it was awful. It felt worse than any moment in my life, not including when my first wife, Suzan, had died suddenly. I was really alone (I know). I just thought I was alone, though. That's a lot of "alones."

I can imagine God saying, "Well, you've done life your way up to now, so how do you like things now?" It didn't take long for the thought to occur to me that I was going to die if I did not somehow change everything – and I meant everything – about how I thought and what I did. I was thinking it might be time for a complete makeover. I prayed hard that day, like I had never prayed before. I really believed life was over and there was no place to go. This was the moment I am sure God was waiting for. There were no more distractions and God finally had my full, undistracted attention.

On the morning of Saturday, May 7, 2021, I woke up at five a.m. out of a deep sleep. I sat up suddenly in bed, wide awake, and had one clear thought in the front of my mind, almost as if it were an audible voice, it was that clear. I heard or thought the command that I was going to write a book. It was a command, not a request or just a vague thought. I literally jumped out of bed, ran to my desk and began to write.

Now I look back and the past two years have been somewhat surreal. It's almost as if I've awakened from a long sleep or a self-induced coma, like Rip van Winkle, and am now making up for a lot of lost time, a lifetime, as it were. I was blind, like the Apostle Paul, going in the wrong direction in life until the scales fell off, not in one day or week, but over the journey that began four, almost five years ago.

At my age, and considering my experiences, I have come to understand that nothing matters more in this life than a person's soul, the question of eternity, and the individual's answer to the question, *what is the point of life? Where are you gonna go when it's all said and done?* To put it another way, what's the point of our existence, why are we here, and what is our purpose?

God had my full, undivided attention and the answer was this: There are too many distractions in our lives that divert our attention from the one true Point of Life and human existence: The Point is:

God loves us, each one of us, and He wants us to love Him and our neighbors as we love ourselves.

That's it, the truth, the whole truth, and nothing but the truth, so help me God. Sounds like I was in a courtroom and on trial. Perhaps I was on trial. Proclaiming the real Point, the only true Point in life, is now my purpose and mission for the rest of my life as was revealed to me early that morning in May. I only wish I had realized this much earlier in life, and I pray I will do it well.

The answer you come up with can save your life, the lives of your family, your loved ones, and influence everyone you come in contact with for the rest of your life. Is the answer important? That would be a resounding YES!

Here's my first confession. Hello, my name is Chad and I'm an axx-hole. Actually, all men are that thing I just mentioned, but some are in recovery. Whether a man is or is not in recovery is "in the eye of the beholder" (i.e., usually their spouse, significant other, or family and friends). I consider myself to now be in some level of recovery, but I was not for most of my life. At times I just thought I was in recovery, but no, based on results, I definitely was not. I still ask those important in my life for affirmation because it's something I will always be working on.

I am now in a place where I can tell my story because I have a mission and purpose to save others the pain and avoid the heartache of dealing with broken relationships, missed opportunities, or painful and destructive addictions. But the most important thing I want no one to miss out on is a personal relationship with our Creator, the living God through his son Jesus Christ and our helper, the Holy Spirit. If you get only one thing from reading this book it is going to be the relationship everyone can have with God. Having the knowledge that He loves all of us, and that all He desires is for us to love Him and to love our neighbors, and that means everyone on this planet other than yourself.

A solitary journey gives plenty of time to reflect on many things. In general, isolation is bad, especially for men, but it affects women negatively also. Solitude is different. Yes, you are alone but with intent. The intent is to gain insight, reflect on experiences, make sense of situations, or just ask why. I chose to use the past five years to ask God a lot of questions. And then the critical element is to listen, listen in the silence for answers. You won't receive answers to all your questions, but you can receive answers, or enlightenment, to the questions you need at the moment. Remember, God does not give you more than you need at any one moment. God will show you what you need at the moment in whatever situation you are in that enables you to fulfill His plan for you. There is no one ever born that could or can handle the wisdom of the universe. Your head would explode like in some cartoon.

You can't "fix" anything in life. You, however, choose how you handle life. You can react or respond. You can live life proactively by not reacting to what life throws at you. Zig Ziglar, the well-known author and speaker, said often "You can only decide if you will **react** or if you will **respond** to circumstances." But you can't fix anything. Fixing stuff refers to repairing a broken leg on a chair, replacing the alternator in your car, or a doctor fixing your broken leg, but you can't fix situations or circumstances in life. Fix'n a relational issue is strictly a concept only a foolish man would think could be accomplished (just ask a woman).

Life happens and then moves on. Time does not stop for anyone. You've heard about a very smart guy by the name of Einstein and how he came up with something called the theory of relativity and the space-time continuum. Without going into details, time is always moving away, never stopping, and sometimes moving faster or slower, replete with black holes, but always moving.

But life happens, and as mortal beings our lives are subservient to this theory. You can't fix it, but you can only choose to react or respond. If you choose "react," you will always be on the defensive. Life will come at you in a vicious onslaught and you will be trapped in a cycle of reacting to circumstances, putting out one fire after another. If you've ever fought a forest fire or grass fire, you know that when you put out one set of flames two or three more will pop up. But "respond" and you can move forward and grow. React and you will only be treading water in life, then eventually grow tired and drown, and something like that was happening to me. Responding means you prepare for what will come or simply deciding that you will not panic and react when confronted with the stuff life throws at you, good and bad. Life doesn't care because it's impersonal. It's just time moving on.

Responding means living intentionally instead of reacting and living by default. I've been reacting to life and living by default for most of my life. If someone asked me what my purpose in life was, I could not tell them. A friend and pastor years ago told me his purpose. Jim Lewis told me that *"he was just a beggar telling other beggars where to find the bread."* It would not be until many years later that I would understand the full meaning and impact of his statement.

Distractions

My purpose from that moment is to tell everyone the truth about the distractions that keep us from knowing God's truth, the consequences of not dealing with distractions, and sharing the knowledge that we can eliminate distractions and live the abundant life God has promised.

What's the point? I'm a sinner, you're a sinner, we're all sinners, and we have become addicted to sin of all kinds. The villain in this story is Satan, who uses lies and distractions to prevent us from seeing the truth that God loves us, He loves everyone, and all He wants is for us to love Him and love our neighbors as ourselves, and that means everyone in the world.

You can reduce and control the not-so-bad distractions, but you can eliminate the useless and bad distractions. We have to stop lying to ourselves. The easiest person for me to lie to is, well, me, and for you, be honest, it's you! We cannot lie to God because He knows our every thought, so He is the only one we can ask for help. This is simply said, but not easy in practice.

Lack of a relationship with God dooms us and is insanity. Insanity, according to Albert Einstein, is defined as "doing the same things over and over again but expecting different results." You have heard the saying that not knowing and understanding history means history will repeat itself. I am a history buff, have been fascinated with it, and this statement is true in one sense, but just knowing history will not change the future except in this sense: knowing and understanding history can mean individual futures can be changed, not the larger future of mankind. That future is preordained and the end a given from God's perspective. He has told us how the story ends but many of us don't accept His word because we still want to act like God and have control of everything, including the future.

So, here we go....

In the morning of May of 2019 I was sitting there, looking into the unknown and dark future for myself, and understanding that the mindset I had and operated from most of my life was the purest definition of insanity. I realized in that moment that I could not continue to think the same way and act the same way, expecting different results. I had reached rock bottom and I didn't like the look or smell of it.

I realized on that day in May that a new future for me would mean changing everything about the way I thought and acted. My first step was practical. Without much thought I decided to create a budget. A silly thought, given that I had always disliked budgets in both my business and personal life. I realized in those dark moments that it had always been an accountability issue for me. I was finally facing this fact and I forced myself to accept being accountable for everything starting with my finances. (Big Jim, if you are listening, I am sure you are laughing yourself silly.)

Change Starts With Simple Steps....Make Your Bed Every Morning

In addition to constructing a budget spreadsheet where I could log all my expenses and income, I decided, without thinking really, to make my bed every morning. Later, someone told me that there is a book titled *Make Your Bed – Little things that change your life....and maybe the world*, written by William H. McRaven. I had never heard of the book, I just started doing little things that would change the way I had been doing things. I have since read the book and it sits on my bedside chest as a reminder every day.

This book will tell parts of my story beginning at a young age up to now, and my relationship with God along the way, the experiences that should have taught me lessons, and how I began to understand in retrospect what it all means. The point being that the path to an abundant life is laid out for us if we will accept some basic truths (which I didn't) and begin to clear out the clutter and distractions the world throws at us. Seeing the confusion I lived with, recognizing the problems both internal and external, and understanding the solutions, can help everyone in their journey through life.

I will tell my story throughout the book with the missed clues and lessons along the way. My story, I hope, will illustrate the distractions that helped me miss the point, and the decades of life I missed out on God's blessings and the abundant life. Moreover, it will also point out the impact my life had on those around me.

The Fearlessness of Foolishness

My story tracks the life of someone who had plenty of opportunities to get it right but never thought any of it applied to him or was qualified to claim them. I never believed that the clues God was leaving for me were meant for me because I didn't believe that God loved me and I did not love myself or my neighbors. I did a lot of crazy things in my life, ages 17 to 27 were my most foolish years. I had then what I now call the condition I have coined "the Fearlessness of Foolishness." This is the belief that I could do anything but if I didn't hurt anyone (that I was aware of), in the end I would be OK and life would turn out alright because I thought I was a "good guy." I also believed myself indestructible, nothing could hurt me, plus it didn't matter. My life's goals didn't include living beyond 35.

The Point is the Purpose of Life

There is only one purpose for human existence: God created you, God loves you, He loves everybody and all He wants in return is for us to love Him and each other, because He knows that doing so will benefit us and lead us to the abundant life He has promised.

I will introduce you to a number of concepts that may be new to you, maybe not. First, as in all great stories, there is a hero. The hero of this story is you, the reader. You are the person who can win in the end. I am going to show you through my story that you are not alone, wherever in life you are now. I will show you how we all face distractions that hide the real purpose in life and how we can beat them.

I will introduce you to the problems, external, internal, and philosophical, we all are faced with. Then I will reveal the source of all of these issues. If you are not a believer in Jesus now, you may deny that Satan exists, but you may not hold that belief when you are finished reading.

A few of you may recognize the formula I am following and I am happy to give credit to Donald Miller and his book *Story Brand*. The book is in the acknowledgements at the end, along with other resources and suggested reading. If I do a good job, and tell a good story, we all win. After all, we were all born to win, as a great philosopher once said (Zig Ziglar).

The Abundant Life

The ultimate goal of this book is to reveal the result of recognizing the obstacles, the problems, the sources of those problems, and the solutions. The result is to achieve the abundant life that God has promised all who believe can enjoy now, here on earth, not just in eternity. The abundant life is there for all to have, if we just follow the instructions that God has given to us.

The point of life is not about our comfort and happiness. It's not about success, possessions, or riches. It's a brick road or a bed of roses. Life will still throw haymakers at you, but you will be able to keep your perspective and respond rather than react. The abundant life is all about not going it alone or figuring it out on your own. It is doing life with help from the Creator of the universe and the power that comes from God. You will never be alone when you are living the abundant life within the will of God, much deeper than shallow desires or wishes. The point is fulfillment. After all, you will never see a hearse on the way to the cemetery pulling a trailer behind it. You are taking nothing out of this life except your soul. The point is fulfillment of a different kind. Fulfillment comes to us in the form of the abundant life, sharing and leading others to it (and I will repeat myself sometimes because it's important). But remember, regardless of how much I talk about the abundant life, it is not a yellow brick road.

I shared a portion of this book with some family members recently, before anyone else has seen or read anything, and their response to it told me clearly who I am writing this book for. I am writing this for them, my family, because they are my neighbors closest to me; then everyone else, because they are a part of my larger family that includes you and all others. Sounds corny, but life sometimes can be that. Someone close to me once said that if what you are writing sometimes brings you to tears, then what you are writing is powerful. This book has brought the tears to my eyes a number of times, and I hope it will be as meaningful to you as it has been for me.

So, in my mission to help others avoid the crucial mistakes I made, I am writing this book. I apologize in advance if anyone gets upset when I seem to be preaching or pontificating, but when someone wakes up after a long sleep and truly sees what's going on around him, a person has gotta say something. Just say'n.

P.S. I want to add this, now that I have finished the book and am ready to hand it off to the publisher. The abundant life I talk about is not someplace to go when we die, but that's the concept I had always held about Heaven. The abundant life is really just Heaven on earth, the Kingdom of God here and now. As one of my pastors, Paul Basden, says, "Heaven begins where the earth ends and your feet begin." Scripture teaches us that Heaven begins when earth stops. The Kingdom of God is right where you are if you believe.

Chapter One
WHY DID I WRITE THIS BOOK AND WHY SHOULD YOU CARE?

"We're on a mission from God." (Elwood J. Blues)

My purpose in writing this book is to leave a trail of breadcrumbs for others to follow. Jim Lewis, a former pastor and large influence in my life, used to say that he was "just a beggar telling other beggars where to find the bread."

My story is one of trying to live up to the expectations of other people, believing that I could intellectually find my path in life, seeking the road to happiness and not finding a purpose, a mission, or true contentment in my life. As a result, life has been chaotic, disoriented, aimless and just reactionary. I was not living intentionally but reacting to what life threw at me. This impacted my life, my family's life, and everyone who had to work with me. It lessened what could have been a positive impact on others into no impact or a negative one. I retreated to live "in my head," and lived focused inward instead of outward.

Are you just "reacting" to what life throws at you?

Zig Ziglar had an audio program called "Goals, Don't be a Wandering Generality." I recorded it, wrote a manual, duplicated thousands of copies, and sold it at seminars all over the country. I also realized later that I had misspelled it on the cover and duplicated hundreds of sets before I spotted the error. The error was that I had printed "Wondering" on the cover instead of the intended "Wandering." However, since the error was inconsequential to the point Zig was making, nobody noticed it. Without a goal you are going to get what you have planned on - nothing. You simply will continue reacting to what life sends your way. As close as I was to the truth, I simply missed it. I missed a lot of great stuff in my seventeen years working with Zig and being in the family. I was a wandering (and wondering) generality.

The light goes on: On Saturday, May 8, 2022, I woke up suddenly out of a dead sleep at 5:00 am and sat up in bed with the crystal clear thought that I had to write a book about my life's experience with distractions and how it has kept me from a close personal relationship with God and everybody else for my entire life. Now, I have had God speak audibly only once in my life. I have had clear communication a few other times, but they were more like a firm prodding that I had to do something but not as clear as this particular Saturday morning. I jumped out of bed and immediately began writing on one of my computers. Six weeks later I had over 10,000 words written.

Bob Goff, a speaker, author, and philanthropist, wrote a book titled *Undistracted*. It caught my attention several weeks after I woke up with this book in mind. I was going to title my book *Distractions* and I had decided to do a search for books with the same theme. It approaches the subject from the aspect of getting rid of distractions and back to what's important in life.

I don't want to expound on a theme someone else has already written about. I want to show all the generations living now that nothing is permanent – not failure, not mediocrity, and not success. My approach is how distractions have affected my life and the lives of those close to me. I want to shed light on the personal price I paid, and you will too if you don't recognize and take control of the distractions that we live with every day. My point is The Point.

What's The Point?

What is the reason for our human existence? The Point is that God created us and wants a relationship with everyone He has created. We sinned in the garden and the penalty for sin is death. That was the reason for sacrifices in the Old Testament. They were an atonement for sin. God sent His Son, Jesus, to die for our sins which prevent a relationship with a Holy God.

I am a sinner; I sin every day and hate it. I am telling you this because I know if you are aware of your sin, you hate it too. And that feeling of hate toward ourselves for sinning causes us to seek more distractions.

> **I am a sinner; I sin every day and hate it. I am telling you this because I know if you are aware of your sin, you hate it too.**

If you hate it too, listen to me and cut it out! Cut out and pare down the distractions and find the life that God wants you to have.

My lack of a personal relationship with God caused me to not reveal myself completely to anyone. I believed that no one would like me if I did. Not living an authentic, genuine, and transparent life cheated everyone around me – but especially me! This included God. I did not have a personal relationship with God the entire time I professed my belief in Him and had accepted Jesus as my Lord and Savior.

My story is not unique. Someone, perhaps many, has lived the same journey and is searching for a way out of the fog that envelops their life. It will destroy a person, a family, and a community around them. If it doesn't destroy, it will rob the joy, the success, and the fulfillment of an abundant life.

I am sitting in my one bedroom apartment as I write. I have lived here alone for three years, separated from my wife of 23 years. She told me in April of 2019 that she did not want to be married to me anymore and I don't blame her now. I was at the proverbial brick wall. Nowhere to go, nobody to blame, and no one, I thought, who could save me. I made the only decision I could. I decided I had to make dramatic changes in my life, not to fix or bail me out of the situation I found myself in, but to have any chance to change the outcome of my life and the lives of others I cared about.

Now for the punchline to what is no joke.

Keep it Simple – K.I.S.S. (Keep It Simple S-----)

All of human existence can be boiled down to this:

1. God created us in His own image and loves all of us: you, me, and everyone.

2. We turned to sin, we continue to sin, we are addicted to sin, and the punishment for sin is death.

3. God sent His Son, Jesus, to die and atone for our sins so we can have a relationship with a Holy God.

4. Satan was given temporary dominion over our world by God, only until Jesus returns.

5. Satan is the father of lies and distractions are among the most useful weapons in his toolbox to keep us from believing that God loves us, Jesus died for our sins, and we can have a personal relationship with God.

6. This is the Truth, the whole Truth, so help me God, and this is the reason I wrote this book.

I want to show you how distractions divert our attention from keeping the main thing the main thing. The things in the way of a personal relationship with God are distractions, all the many, many distractions in our lives.

The past three years have been at the same time the worst of my life and the best of my life. I have spent most of my time reflecting on every moment of my life up to now and I continue to do so. I have sought Christian-based psychological counseling, weekly visits with a Biblical counselor, and an awesome, intense ten-week program called "Rooted" through my church. Much has been revealed to me about my journey to a place of complete brokenness and the transformation that has led me out of that dark place.

I wrote this book with the hope it will explain and make clear that no matter what situation or circumstance you are facing there is a way, a chance to strip away the nonsense, the distractions in your life, and get to an amazing place, the abundant life God promises to all of us who believe.

Growing Up in Post-war America

I grew up in a middle class family in Connecticut, New Jersey, and Michigan. Dad worked in the insurance industry after a long stint in the Army starting just before World War II began and ending about a year after the war ended. Mom was a stay-at-home mom in those days. I was born in Albany, New York, and we moved to Guilford, Connecticut, about age four. Mom was anxious to get me into school so she could concentrate on my brother, Kirk, who was three years younger than I. So, off to kindergarten I went at age four.

We attended church at an Episcopal church in Guildford. It is a beautiful, old stone traditional church with a red front door on the Village Green in the center of town. About all I remember about church and God in those years was the annual visit from the parish priest to talk with Mom and Dad about the annual giving campaign. I also sang in the boys choir and was an acolyte or altar boy. We moved as I was about to begin the sixth grade.

We lived there until I was nine, and then moved closer to New York City for about six months when Dad changed jobs while Mom and Dad shopped for a house in New Jersey. I can't remember attending any church in the brief time we lived in Stamford, but I began sixth grade while there.

I'm pretty sure this may not seem exciting to some, but I'm trying to paint a picture of the world I grew up in. I never considered writing a book, even after spending close to 20 years in the personal and corporate development industry publishing, designing, and selling lots of books by other people. I always figured that other people had more important stuff to say in a book than I did. I always told others that "You write it, I'll get it published, printed and sold," or something to that effect.

When we finally moved to New Jersey, I finished the sixth grade and began the seventh grade. It was the first of Mom and Dad's "quaint" old homes that we lived in. They had an interest in "quaint and unique" homes all throughout my growing up and later. Moving around like we did because of Dad's career gave me the impression I was an outsider, and I felt like I was just observing life but not a real part of what was going on around me. This is probably when I started living in my own head with lots of fantasy and inward thoughts. I learned to keep my real thoughts to myself and not reveal my true self to anyone. I had no really close friends, although I certainly tried to fit in with everybody. I was smaller than everybody else, even the girls in class. I didn't start to grow taller until I was in the later years of high school.

Unique and *houses with history* meant we didn't live in town where I would have plenty of friends to play with. We lived 3.5 miles out of town and away from my school. The driveway wasn't paved, so no basketball. One girl near my age lived 100 yards up the road. Lynn was my only playmate but we found plenty to do. We lived on 10 acres with a river, an island, and lots of woods that included a swamp. We also had Schooley's Mountain behind us, and winter was super fun sledding and skiing down the mountain road. There were no other kids to play with anywhere nearby and the isolation did a lot to hinder my emotional development.

All these observations I have made in hindsight of the past three years. During those early years, and for many years thereafter, I had no idea how my circumstances contributed to my development. God was a disembodied concept that didn't have a direct impact or meaning in my life. Life was solely reacting to what life sent my way, and that's what the rest of life had in store for me.

> **Life was solely reacting to what life sent my way, and that's what the rest of life had in store for me.**

My beloved grandfather died when I was ten years old. He gave me unconditional love more than anyone else in my family. Mom and Dad loved me, but they were the parental units (as we labeled them in the '60s). Grandpa was magical. He knew how to fix everything and he knew everything. Holidays and summer vacations were awesome and looked forward to all year. Then he died when I was ten. In those days, certainly in our family, children were not included in any of the important matters of life. I was not allowed to attend his funeral and no one ever explained anything to a ten-year-old boy who had lost his beloved grandpa. This one event affected me for many, many years.

Now, to let you understand that Grandpa was not superhuman and one of the effects he had on my life was not the best, let me tell you this small fact. Grandpa had a big, high bed that was fun to jump on in his bedroom. I did bounce off twice and broke my collarbone once. But the fascinating thing for a ten-year-old boy in that bedroom, and in his nightstand specifically, was a stack of *Playboy* magazines. This will show up later in my life.

I hope by now you, as the reader and seeker, understand that everybody has a story. The details vary but the details all have the effect of shaping our lives. They shape our personalities, reactions or responses, likes and dislikes, and the results shape our lives and the lives of those around us. Scary, isn't it?

Now all you have to do is to accept this, admit the truth, and begin to understand how you came to be where and what you are now. Now is all that matters. The past is done, and the future awaits you and everyone else you know and love. Changes and commitments you make today will influence how you live tomorrow, but tomorrow is out of your control. It boils down to how you will respond to what the future brings.

This book you are reading and the concepts contained herein have the capacity to set you free – if you will allow yourself to believe, believe in God's promises in His Word, and have the faith that God loves you, He loves everyone, and He forgives all who believe in Jesus as the Savior Who died instead of us for our sins. Then you can understand and believe that Satan does not have the power to distract you from God's love, His promises, and the abundant life God promises all who believe.

This is the whole point of human existence, the only point. I will repeat: God loves us, all of us; we have all sinned and the penalty for sin is death; Jesus died to atone for our sins so we can have a relationship with a Holy God; Satan has only temporary dominion in our world; the father of lies uses distractions to distract us from God; this is the truth, the whole truth, so help me God. This is the reason I wrote this book.

Chapter Two

HYPOCRISY: MANAGING IMAGE OR FORMING CHARACTER

"Hypocrisy: Spending time managing your image and very little time forming your character."
(Jim Johnson, Senior Pastor, Preston Trail Community Church)

I will explain how distractions are related to purpose and mission. Distractions in your life, if you are honest with yourself (I know, hard to do), benefit your image more than your character. This is fairly normal, especially in the times we live in now.

If you spend time managing your image and little time forming your character, you do not have time to develop your purpose, let alone a life's mission. Do you know your purpose and do you have a mission?

We begin adding distractions to our life at an early age. Today they are all around us and way too easy to start filling out our lives with distractions that lead us to managing image instead of building character. It was a lot easier in times past to not let distractions blur our purpose because there were far fewer distractions in decades past. There were no cell phones, Internet, social media, general affluence, and all the stuff we acquire and worry about. As we acquire possessions like clothes, cars, and houses, we worry about them, don't we? The more you have, the more you have to manage. We have fear of losing our jobs and how we can afford our cars, our homes, and our entire lifestyle.

> **As we acquire possessions like clothes, cars, and houses, we worry about them, don't we? The more you have, the more you have to manage.**

I have just seen a commercial for a new reality television show about digital addictions and intervention to help people get unhooked from their electronic devices. Go figure. I do believe, after watching two generations of young people over recent years, that digital addictions can have a similar social impact as other addictions and distractions, although the physical impact is less.

I grew up in the aftermath of World War II and the Korean War. The 1950s and '60s were unique. The world was recovering from a world-wide catastrophe, rebuilding economies and lives. America emerged from the wars with the only intact and fully functioning economy in the world. As such, we took the lead in helping to rebuild a large portion of the world. I think my fascination with history began at an early age mainly because Dad brought a lot of stuff home from his service during World War II. He served in the Pacific during the battle of Okinawa and later during the Korean occupation. He brought home stuff like weapons, his army equipment, uniforms and helmets and such. I played a lot with all that stuff. The other aspect of the '50s was that television in that period had a lot of shows with subject matter of World War II and the Korean War, not to mention all the cowboy western themed shows. Vietnam hadn't happened yet and we had no idea what was coming.

My family life was amazing. My father worked in the insurance industry and was still very involved in a military career in the army reserves. I thought it was cool that he was a high ranking officer and spent several weeks every summer working at the Pentagon in Washington, D.C. We got to go to Washington for a week every summer for years.

My mother was a stay-at-home mom in the early years before becoming involved, very successfully, in real estate. In fact, this became an issue between Mom and Dad as I was later to learn. Mom became so successful she was soon earning more than Dad was as the chief operating officer of several very large insurance companies.

God still did not occupy much of my attention. Sundays were a ritual of Sunday school, then church with the family, then home for a formal Sunday dinner that Mom would prepare. Formal and very ritual.

We were members of the Episcopal church, which adhered to the "high Episcopal" style of observance. We attended church every Sunday we were in town. The exceptions were vacations, which were usually visiting Syracuse, New York, where grandparents, uncles, aunts and cousins on my mother's side of the family lived. A few vacations would take us to Lancaster County, Pennsylvania, or Rochester, New York, where Dad's side of the family lived.

I remember the yearly visit from the parish priest to talk with Mom and Dad about their annual giving commitment or tithe to the church. I know I spoke of this previously, but it represented a little boy's perspective of God and church. Today that practice seems odd, but it was at that time "old school" church business.

I was an acolyte or altar boy and a member of the boys choir. That meant lighting the candles, walking in the processional to begin and end the services, and assisting with communion. I believed in God, but really had no understanding of Who He was, what He had done for us, or what we were expected to do for our part. It was just ceremony and ritual to me. I really didn't give it much thought. I was more interested in baseball cards, bicycles, BB guns, comic books, and playing in the dirt.

Mom and Dad never spoke much about God or what God meant to them. The rules of society as we learned were: don't discuss religion, politics, or sex at the dinner table or in any company, including our family. However, I did learn a lot about girls from the guys at school. The lessons I learned from Mom and Dad were that there were certain ways to behave, speak, dress, and all around how to conduct ourselves because, after all, "What would people think?" I was being trained to be superficial, to maintain a face through which no one could see the real me.

> **I was being trained to be superficial, to maintain a face through which no one could see the real me.**

The eras of the '50s and '60s were all about "more." Mom and Dad's business and social circles were all related to moving up socially and economically. All their friends were already in higher social strata or were on their way there. I did become fascinated with history during these years. History, as I came to realize, explained a lot about how the world worked at large. It explained why people and nations did what they did. It also, I realized, predicted how they would act in the future.

New Jersey soon gave way to Michigan. Dad accepted a job managing the Ford Motor Company's insurance subsidiary, American Roads Insurance. My sophomore, junior, and half of my senior years in high school were in Birmingham and Bloomfield Hills, Michigan. I did make more friends here and had more fun. It really was a major issue for me when Dad said we were moving again halfway through my senior year, and it was not good. I even had a girlfriend by that time.

I don't remember much about church or God during those years. There were a lot more distractions. I did get very involved with the Boy Scouts, because my little brother joined and I was encouraged to join to look after him. I really enjoyed it and had a great time. The Boy Scouts were sponsored by our church, but I still can't remember anything about church except the name, St. James Episcopal.

High school gave way eventually to college. I didn't want to go, but Dad had a way of convincing me. He got me up one morning in time to see the garbage truck come by. Dad pointed out the guy riding on the back of the truck and jumping off to pick up the cans to empty them in the back of the truck. He said that without a college degree I could only expect to have a job like that. I apologize to all sanitation workers for that, but it did motivate me enough to agree to try college.

The Fearlessness of Foolishness

College was like turning on the lights in a dark room. I was welcomed into a fraternity and it was party time. Planning parties that were better than the last one or anyone else's party became a specialty of mine. I enjoyed the camaraderie, friendship, and seemingly a purpose in my life. However, after five years and very close to graduating I became distracted, bored, and ready to quit, without any goals in mind. The summer of 1971 I went up to the Adirondacks to help my great aunt Maggie run her business after my great uncle Harry passed away just after Christmas that year. While there, Mom called to tell me I had a letter from the draft board and my summer without a goal was over.

God was not even a tiny thought. I was navigating life on my own. I was too self-absorbed to realize that I was not doing a very good job. I felt privileged, and life would turn out fine in my view. I had no clue as to how that would happen but I was confident. Growing up, Mom had plied me with tales of our family ancestors. She was big on genealogy and had heard all the tales at the feet of her grandmother. One of the tales she told was that we were descendants of Dutch royalty several generations back, and it gave me a feeling that I was a prince – or something.

I went for my draft physical and passed, of course. It was 1971 and the Vietnam war was still raging, and everyone who got drafted had a good chance to end up in Vietnam in some capacity. That was when I opened one eye and decided to take some measure of control of my life. I hurriedly went to all the armed forces recruiters to see what options were available.

The Army had only a tank crewman or military policeman available; the Navy guaranteed at least one year at sea immediately; the Coast Guard had a one year waiting list; the National Guard had no slots at all, but the U.S. Air Force had an all-expense paid vacation tour available and I wouldn't even need to cut all my hair off. Wow, I didn't hesitate to sign on for the tour. Just like a normal job, regular hours, etc., and off I went to basic training. After basic and technical school I was assigned my first station in Big Springs, Texas.

I was just warming up. God was certainly not in the forefront of my life, although I walked by the base chapel every day on the way to work. Maybe I thought God only lived inside a building. I didn't know any Christians that I was aware of. Nobody talked about God, that I can remember.

Then, nearing the end of my first year tour at Webb AFB, I received orders for Germany! It sounded like it could be a lot of fun. Just after a Christmas leave I headed to Germany and Rhein-Main AFB. I had no idea what to expect, but I believed the possibilities were endless. The Air Force would give me purpose and mission in my life and I would not have to think much, so I didn't. I really didn't have much structure except when I was at work. I played fastpitch softball on the base team and traveled a lot throughout Europe. I had no other duties or details because I played on a "varsity" team and the wing commander was a sports nut. Other than that, we had a lot of free time for "other endeavors."

No Accountability

And that opens another story of my entrepreneurial and recreational escapades. I was at a point where I felt no accountability other than the Air Force, and they didn't seem to care as long as I showed up promptly for work, looked sharp, and carried out my assigned duties. This lack of accountability is a disease afflicting many, then as now. My barracks were right across the street from the NCO club, and as an NCO I took advantage of the inexpensive alcohol in excessive quantities. My friends and I grew tired of that quickly and realized that drugs were readily available everywhere. So, with the entrepreneurial spirit of an American, my buddy and I were quick to see that the math worked a whole lot better if we purchased our supplies in quantity, sold much of it, and what was left was ours to consume for basically free!

I quickly realized that most of the airmen spent most of their paychecks within the first week after payday, then they were broke for another week or so. I can't remember if we were paid bi-monthly or every two weeks, but it doesn't matter. Since I had sold them something that was partially responsible for their being broke, and I had lots of cash on hand, I was more than happy to loan them money until they got paid again. Then, on payday, they would pay me back. No one ever failed to pay me, as they knew there would be no loans or "stuff" in the future if they didn't. Payday was known as "Mother's Day" because it was the day to pay that "mother f....r." Oh, did I mention that I charged only a "nominal" 50% interest for my services?

I also knew many of the guys who didn't smoke or drink on base. Overseas, the military had a Class VI store where alcohol and tobacco were sold without any taxes charged in the price. So, alcohol and cigarettes were really cheap. I would park my car around the corner from the store, give money to the guys who would then go into the store, purchase the goods using their ration cards, and bring their purchases out to deposit in the trunk of my car. At that time, I leased an apartment on the top floor of a highrise in town and paid most of my rent with a couple of gallons of bourbon. It seems that bourbon was not available in the German economy and my landlord really liked Jim Beam.

Well, that really covers most of my military career. I didn't give much thought to the right or wrong of my actions. It was just good fun and we could get away with it with impunity. Mom and Dad taught me well how to maintain a good front or public image. I looked good, clean haircut, starched uniform, and proper military bearing, so no one ever looked at me twice. Bottom line was that I was living a life without many boundaries. I was not accountable to anyone if I kept up appearances, looked sharp, and walked straight.

I managed my image and kept the real person locked up tight inside. God was not a factor in my life. I was a nice guy, in my mind, but I really was a runaway train speeding into the future. I had no purpose, no goals, and no mission in life. I still thought life would turn out fine, somehow, because I was tall, handsome, somewhat educated and an American.

There I go, putting up a front, managing my image. I'm still afraid to say tall, white, and male to account for my feeling that everything in my life would turn out fine. It's true, but I didn't realize it then. I had no concept of the racism and sexism in our society at the time. I had not grown up around anyone of color until the Air Force, where I had the opportunity to become close friends and work with many who became good friends. And although I grew up in the fifties and sixties when women were shut out of well-paying and meaningful jobs, I really accepted women in uniform without a second thought. I would say now I was so self-centered that I was unaware of what was going on around me.

If I had been more aware during those years, I also would have realized that God was always there. In spite of the foolish and dangerous things I was doing, He protected me. There were many times that events could have gone sideways but didn't. On the other hand, I still was wandering through life without purpose or mission.

Chapter Three
LIFE GETS IN THE WAY

Now some bad news: How are we distracted from what's important?

Life gets in the way. Distractions.

If you are in the react mode and just dealing with life as it comes at you down the stream of time, you will encounter thousands or maybe millions of distractions. How you deal with them determines your success or failure, your happiness or discontent.

Distractions come in many forms. Often they appear to be of little consequence but later develop into bigger issues. It's like the old southern tale of how to boil a bullfrog. If you were to try and plunge a bullfrog into boiling water, it would be very hard as the bullfrog would fight frantically and try to stay out of the water. He probably would jump right out. However, if you put the bullfrog into barely warm water he would sit there and enjoy the feeling. Then you could turn up the heat slowly and he would just keep enjoying the warm, cozy feeling until it was too late and he was cooked. Distractions have innocuous beginnings.

I left the Air Force on December 7th (Pearl Harbor Day). I was flown to McGuire AFB and processed for separation, given travel expenses to my HOR or Home of Record, $5. It seems that my home address was about 30 miles from McGuire when I enlisted, but Mom and Dad had moved to the Chicago area while I was overseas. Well, the problem was that I had spent all of my money before I left Germany and didn't have enough to buy an airline ticket to Chicago. How's that for not thinking ahead? The Air Force did give me a free bus ride to the Philadelphia airport, however, but I had to call Dad from the airport and ask him to buy a ticket so I could come home. He did, thankfully.

My discharge a few months short of a four-year enlistment was the result of my request for an early release to return to college. After a short stay with Mom and Dad at their home and buying a new van, I hit the road to Oklahoma City to enroll back in school. I did really well back in school for two semesters, much better than my previous tenure with college. However, I was still a man without a purpose or mission in life, and getting bored and restless again.

Chris, one of my fraternity brothers, had gotten out of the Marines at the same time I did the Air Force. He owned a house and he invited me to share it with him. We reconnected with another close friend and fraternity brother, David. David was an entrepreneur and had plans to start an antique importing business with a French partner, Henri. Their plan was to open a "to the trade only" showroom near the Dallas World Trade Center. After consuming a lot of beer with Chris and David, I asked if I could jump in on their deal and they said ok. Maybe it was because only I owned a set of tools. So off to Dallas we went with a semi truckload of antiques from Henri, and the adventure was launched.

We didn't know anything about antiques, business, or Dallas, but off we went. We also didn't know anyone in Dallas, started with no customers, but that didn't faze us. It was an adventure while we made our presence known in town. In the meantime, we all lived in a three bedroom rental house: me, Chris, David and David's wife, Charlotte, plus three dogs. We also ate beans and lived on the edge while we waited for our business to be accepted in the Dallas business community.

Somewhere along the way Chris broke up the band, went back to North Carolina where he grew up, and returned with a wife, Pam. Needless to say, Chris and Pam got their own place. Pam went to work at a high-end linen shop in a small boutique area of shops. Pam happened to work with a girl who Pam thought should meet me and I her. Her name was Suzan. It took Pam and Chris almost three, maybe four months of intensive persuasion and salesmanship for both of us to finally agree to a blind double date with them. And, as they say, the rest is history.

Suzan knocked my socks off. I was so nervous on that first date I consumed way too much alcohol. The drive home was, well, let's just say I don't remember it. I was very excited when Suzan agreed to a second date, and a third and more. I will mention here that before the second date

Suzan asked me a question I didn't understand until later. She asked me if I knew who Zig Ziglar was and my answer was something like "what's that?" or "who?" I had no idea, but, fortunately, that was the answer she was hoping for. She had experienced too many guys asking her for dates only interested in getting close to Zig, who was a well-known sales trainer and motivational speaker already.

We dated for about six months then took a short break while I was given time to decide if I really was "committed to a serious relationship." She mentioned something like "tick tock, the clock is ticking, I'm 28 years old and I need to know if you are serious about our relationship." I took a couple of weeks to make a decision and decided that, yes, I was definitely serious and committed. We got married several months later in August of 1977. I later learned that in the world of sales, when closing a sale you should recognize that the customer's biggest motivator is often that the fear of loss is greater than the desire for gain. So the successful salesperson should add the factor of an impending event, such as *the opportunity to buy is now because the option to buy later will not be available later* and *the time to make the decision is now or never.* I wonder where she learned that?

If you have never watched the movie *Draft Day* starring Kevin Costner as the general manager of the Cleveland Browns, you should. In the later scenes in the draft room there is the perfect example of this sales technique when Costner is making trades on the phone while they are "on the clock" during the NFL draft. You'll know what I mean when you are watching, as Costner makes several stupendous deals using the fear of loss method of making the sale. Much later I realized that my fear of losing amazing Suzan outweighed my desire for anything else in life.

Suzan had reservations about some aspects of my antique business, especially the lack of sufficient income, and she encouraged me to pursue what I really wanted to do and that was restore antiques, not necessarily sell them. Sales is a large part of every business, but I preferred the operational side of things; at that time, dealing with people was not my forté.

I left Orion and opened my own shop on Main Street in downtown Dallas. I was restoring and repurposing antiques for dealers and decorators. Suzan came home one night and said her dad, Zig, had convinced her to try a new sales program he had started. She had quit her job as a server at The Old San Francisco Steak House and she would be calling on stores and businesses to sell books and training programs directly. She said she didn't like doing it after trying it for a couple of weeks. I said I would like to try it, shut down my shop to try sales, and began my 17-plus year career with Zig Ziglar.

I did listen to the tapes and read the book (there was only one at that time), but that didn't take the place of real sales training. Zig's idea of sales training was, "Listen to the tapes and read the books." But I subconsciously liked the idea of somebody paying me a regular paycheck and taking care of the details and everything else. It gave me a purpose, although it was someone else's purpose. Someone else's purpose was ok with me and it was a great purpose.

My life at this point still was a matter of taking on life as it came at me (and us) and reacting to it. No intentional thinking here! Events were just propelling me into the future. God was in control but I wasn't putting any effort toward using my gifts. But I couldn't see that and didn't understand it.

We had moved into my apartment near downtown Dallas after we got married. The Tolltec Apartments were not the greatest place for a wife or family. It was great for a bachelor because it was close to our showroom, night life, and restaurants, but it was "dicey," and definitely not in a good part of town. When we later bought our house in Garland, a suburb of Dallas, while giving our notice prior to moving out, the property manager actually cried, saying "You're the last normal people left here." Moving out to the "burbs" was just another step in the "American Dream." I thought it was expected. Certainly Suzan thought so and I agreed, still just reacting to life.

Reacting to what life presented was a result of being distracted by everything other than what is really important. I was distracted by work, money, house, truck, television, and the Dallas Cowboys. I did not feel that my relationship with Suzan was that important. After all, we were married and I thought that the hard work was over. I had met her, courted her, proposed to her (I think it was me who proposed), and that the rest of life would just flow pleasantly along. Life would be happy and it was "all gud."

What I now find amazing is that in light of my escapades before meeting Suzan, I didn't continue to do drugs, drink to excess, or participate in anything unseemly or illegal. I just thought I was a nice guy and everything would turn out fine in life. Maybe it was a bit of the "do no harm" mentality many are afflicted with. Many people feel that if they don't do anything too terrible, grossly illegal, or hurtful to others, they will end up in life "okay."

Well, for me, distractions were just beginning to multiply. When you are unaware of how our existence truly works, you are at the mercy of events seemingly out of your control. The longer you wait to deal with distractions, the more the enemy knows you are susceptible to them and will throw more your way. Distractions suck the life out of you in more ways than one. Soon, your life is so "busy" with distractions you have no time for the really important things in life. You may not even be aware of what's happening. You won't even know you are being consumed, you just know you don't have time for anything, relationships begin to weaken or fail, anxiety increases, depression may set in, and your life begins to crumble.

> The longer you wait to deal with distractions, the more the enemy knows you are susceptible to them and will throw more your way. Distractions suck the life out of you in more ways than one.

And, the truth be told, most of the distractions aren't "bad." There are just so many that they have the same effect on you, at the end of the day, that a couple of "bad" distractions would have – like drugs, alcohol, or lust.

Kids, sports, television, Internet, exercise, food, cars, homes, clothes, vacations, gadgets, business, success, envy are all innocuous in and of themselves. But most people have a little – if not a lot – of all of these distractions in their lives.

I finally was forced to recognize that I had lots of distractions from outside in my life that I let into my life, and from the inside ones that I manufactured on my own. Once I identified my distractions, then I could begin peeling them away. I was pleasantly surprised with what I could dismiss and do without.

Cutting the television cord not only saved me literally $150 per month, it gave me back three or four hours a day and the new resource of that time allowed me to read books. Reading a physical book in the past was one of my true pleasures. I grew up with Mom and Dad having a large library of the classics of literature, and I enjoyed having a large library of my own before the apartment. In the past year alone I have read a total of 17 books, including one book that was a compilation of 25 letters written by theologians as far back in the history of the church as St. Augustine. I don't think I read more than one book (if that many) before cutting the television off. The experience of reading far exceeded any temporary pleasure I could have had watching television. This is even considering that I normally only watched documentaries and history shows anyway.

Cutting the cord was hard when I thought about not having what I thought was an essential element of modern life. It isn't. I got along fine without television and the huge savings I experienced was very pleasurable. My budget enjoyed the extra $150 a month.

What else is costing you time, energy, money, and diverting you from something in life far more important than watching movies, sports, news, and whatever else you spend time watching or – just having background noise?

Let me talk to you about the news, one of the biggest distractions I know of. It doesn't matter what political persuasion you happen to be, what sociological group you may identify with, what religion or spiritual group you belong to, or ethnic identity you may claim, the news is poison. Reading and obsessing over content of news every day will create anxiety, fear, anger, and all around dissatisfaction with everybody and everything.

Here are the facts about news. The news today is the same as the news 2000 years ago. It's the same today in New York, Dallas, Los Angeles, Moscow, London, Paris, you name it, as it was, as it is, and as it always will be. The fact that news used to take weeks, months, even years to get to us, now takes 30 minutes or even 30 seconds. So what? The same exact issues are news today as they were 2000 or 500 or 100 years ago. It just gets to us faster and provokes our responses sooner. It seems like there's more happening now because it's reported sooner and more often.

Everyone can comment on events within the hour now instead of reading about it or hearing about it by word of mouth days, weeks, months, or even years after the fact. By then, emotions are cold instead of hot. Now we get all exercised about events right away and everything seems to be happening faster, bigger, and more impactful now.

The solution is to not read the news often, seldom, or at all. Just skim reading or surfing through it without becoming angry, fearful, or reactionary if you can't live without it, and just "have" to read or listen to it.

Cut the cable, cancel subscriptions, and avoid glancing at screens wherever you go and you will learn to relax. You will experience far less anxiety, fear, and hatred. I've tried it and I couldn't be happier. My dad in his later years, while I was caring for him, turned on the television when he got up and sat on his sofa watching the news (Fox News) all day long until he went to bed. As a result, he was often irritable, cranky, and highly opinionated. Until I came to essentially live with them he never changed, only getting worse. We had moved to within a block from Mom and Dad so I could care better for them. Then I told him his news time was going to be limited to an hour or two per day. I made him aware of how he reacted to watching news all day long, and that I was not going to put up with either his attitude or having the noise in the background during the six to eight hours a day I was spending in their house.

Life got a lot easier for all of us when that edict was laid down and Dad's attitude improved a whole lot. Mine too.

The world spins and the human story repeats itself every day, everywhere, and will continue until it all comes to an end – and it will. The human story throughout history is repeated constantly and the few islands of hope are where the people of God "love the Lord your God with all your heart and with all your soul and with all your mind (strength). This is the first and greatest commandment. And the second is like it: Love your neighbor as yourself."

Chapter Four

YOU CAN'T DELEGATE YOUR FAITH OR PRAYERS

Life still was a matter of taking life as it came at me and reacting to it. No intentional thinking here! Events were just pushing me into the future. God was in control and I wasn't, but I couldn't see that.

I was married to an amazing woman that God had obviously chosen for me. We had two beautiful children and a great family around us. This is a difficult time in my life to write about because it brings back many memories I haven't completely worked through yet, I guess. However, my daughter, Katherine, is only too happy to help me remember.

Zig's latest book at the time was published, printed, and being sold. *Confessions of a Happy Christian* was his second book, and he had written it with Suzan specifically in mind and said so in the book. He gave her a copy and she put it on a shelf in our apartment without reading it. Some weeks later she got sick, probably just a cold, but she ended up on the sofa and she pulled out the only book in the apartment,

Confessions of a Happy Christian. She didn't put it down until she had finished it. When I came home that evening she had a big smile on her face and tears in her eyes and she said, "I just met Jesus."

We talked, and I told her I was ready to let Jesus be my Savior also. It was like a huge release when I said that. The lights didn't go on or the music didn't play in the background, but I felt a huge release when I asked Jesus into my life. That same night Zig had a speaking event and we both went. I had to work the sales table and Suzy wanted to go so she could tell her dad. She walked up to him and said, "Daddy, I read the book," and he knew she had accepted Jesus. I can't remember seeing a man so happy as Zig was right then. Suzan's brother, Tom, walked up and Zig turned to him and said "Tom, guess who Suzy met tonight?" It was a big night.

That night began a journey for Suzan and me, individually and as a couple, that would lead us through valleys low and mountains high.

Sitting in the Garage will not Make You a Car

Suzan and I set out to find a church home. We had visited church with Zig and Jean many times, but knew we didn't want to drive all the way downtown Dallas to where the rest of the family went. We were friends with a couple, I can't remember how we knew them, but they invited us to Believer's Chapel. We showed up the next Sunday at church, but our friends were not there and we never saw them again. Today I would call that a divine appointment. Believer's Chapel was a great church for new Christians. It taught the Bible in a methodical and systematic way. The pastor, S. Lewis Johnson, was a fantastic expositor and very clear in everything he taught. He used to joke that we wouldn't have to take Christianity 101 when we got to Heaven.

I still didn't get it that God loved even me and all He asked for in return was a relationship with me. I delegated prayer and the God portion of life to Suzan. And of course, Zig and Jean were godly people, and I believed that all that would cover me with God. I was determined to intellectualize and fake my way through life

> I still didn't get it that God loved even me and all He asked for in return was a relationship with me.

Dreams, Italy, and Holland

We purchased our first home in 1979 before our first daughter, Katherine, was born in November of 1979. My fraternity brother, Gary, was our agent and said, "Don't worry about qualifying, I got this. Just sign the papers here." I signed and we moved into a house when I was earning a total of $500 a month and Suzan made about the same as a waitress (I know we call them "servers" now, but then they were waiters and waitresses). Looking back, I'm sure somebody fudged something somewhere. Whatever, we had our own home.

Three years later our second girl, Elizabeth, came along. I never gave a thought about being disappointed she wasn't a boy. I loved her. We were just rolling along until Elizabeth was one year old. Suzan was certain something wasn't right. Elizabeth wasn't developing normally and we went to the doctors for help. After her spending one week in the hospital and the doctors running every test they had in 1980, the diagnosis was, "We don't know what's wrong or how it happened." The diagnosis was "Delayed Development." Nothing more concrete than that, but it did qualify Elizabeth for a lifetime of medical care, therapy, and Social Security benefits. The rest of Elizabeth's story is a story for another time. I will just add right here something that may resonate with other parents of special needs children, maybe who are just starting their journey.

Welcome to Holland

This is a reprint of an article taken from the *Rocky Mountain News*, October 29, 1990.

> *I am often asked to describe the experience of raising a child with a disability –to try to help people who have not shared that unique experience to understand, to imagine how it would feel. It's like this....*
>
> When you're going to have a baby, it's like planning a fabulous vacation trip – to Italy. You buy a bunch of guide-books and make your wonderful plans. The Coliseum, Michelangelo's David, the gondolas in Venice. You may learn some handy phrases in Italian. It's very exciting.
>
> After months of eager anticipation, the day arrives. You pack your bags and off you go. Several hours later, the plane lands. The stewardess comes in and says, "Welcome to Holland."
>
> "Holland?!?!" you say, "What do you mean, Holland? I signed up for Italy! I'm supposed to be in Italy. All my life I've dreamed of going to Italy."

But there's been a change in the flight plan. They've landed in Holland and there you must stay. The important thing is that they haven't taken you to a horrible, disgusting, filthy place, full of pestilence, famine and disease. It's just a different place.

So you must go out and buy new guidebooks. And you must learn a whole new language. And you will meet a whole new group of people you have never met.

It's just a different place. It's slower-paced than Italy, less flashy than Italy. But after you've been there for a while and you catch your breath, you look around, and you begin to notice that Holland has windmills, Holland has tulips, Holland even has Rembrandts.

But everyone you know is busy going to and from Italy, and they're all bragging about what a wonderful time they had there. And for the rest of your life, you will say, "Yes, that's where I was supposed to go. That's what I had planned."

The pain of that will never, ever, ever go away, because the loss of a dream is a very significant loss.

But if you spend your life mourning the fact that you didn't get to Italy, you may never be free to enjoy the very special, the very lovely things about Holland.

I don't know who originally wrote this piece, but for Suzan and me it came to exemplify our journey....to Holland.

As mentioned, I started traveling with Zig to sell books and tape programs in the back of the rooms where he spoke. At some point in the first two years or so, Suzan began to drop hints with first her mom, Jean, and then Zig, that I was traveling too much and it would be nice if he hired someone else to travel some to the speaking engagements. Of course, that began to happen. I began doing more inside work, starting with running the warehouse and shipping departments when I wasn't out with Zig.

The business grew fast and Zig was in great demand as a speaker and trainer. We began to build a training company around him with people who could develop corporate training programs and then a sales team that could sell them. Along came a program for schools and we grew at a fantastic rate. I was determined to make myself useful (and indispensable) in any way I could. We started having quality and supply issues with the recorded programs and I took over recording the programs as Zig spoke. Editing, producing, and duplicating followed. Then we had to expand our footprint and we moved into new digs.

We built a new recording studio, duplication and fulfillment facility called At The Top Cassettes after the title of Zig's first book. In addition, we added an in-house training facility and office space for the over seventy associates we grew to employ.

Sat Next to the Fire but Never Got Warm

Throughout my time with Zig Ziglar professionally, and as a family member, I had the incredible opportunity to meet and spend time with some pretty fantastic people: authors, speakers, pastors, and outstanding individuals from all walks of life. I can't even begin to name them without missing many. The wealth of knowledge and experience embodied by these people was off the charts. Yet, I did not gain the insights that would have enriched my life, my family's lives, and the lives of many others from this fantastic opportunity. I gained some, of course, but I never realized how privileged I was to be that close to the accumulated wisdom and insights that I was being exposed to.

I have met Robert Schuller, Bob Goff, Brian Tracy, Bernie Lofchick, Ike Reighard, W.A Criswell, John Maxwell, Todd Duncan, Les Brown, Ken Blanchard, Fred Smith, Sr., Denis Waitley, Charlie "Tremendous" Jones, Tom Hopkins, and Tony Jeary, just to name a few.

At every speaking engagement to which I accompanied Zig, there were people who were sponsors, leaders, and just great people who just wanted to help others, grow others, and make their community better. My life was enriched by all of these people. The sad part was that I was not aware enough, at the time, to take all this influence in my life and grow as a person. What a difference it would have made to my family, my colleagues, and my own life if I had taken what was given me and built upon it. Ah, well…

> I thought I was doing well, but I was not a happy man. I harbored feelings of inadequacy I now recognize as the "imposter syndrome." I was an insecure person inside while managing a false image of a capable man on the outside. Those feelings grew with every success professionally.

All the while we were growing as a business. My responsibilities grew to eventually become the senior vice president or chief operating officer. I thought I was doing well, but I was not a happy man. I harbored feelings of inadequacy I now recognize as the "imposter syndrome." I was an insecure person inside while managing a false image of a capable man on the outside. Those feelings grew with every success professionally.

Second Knock on the Door

In 1994 Suzan began to feel something was wrong and she went to see her doctor. The news was devastating. She had a condition with no known cause and no cure, Pulmonary Fibrosis. The only treatment was a regimen of steroids and if and when the condition deteriorated, a double lung transplant. Suzan passed away a year later in May 1995 and the world came crashing down. Everyone was crushed. But the amazing thing was Suzan's attitude was different. She became much, much closer to God. And I didn't. I began to feel punished. First Elizabeth with her issues and now Suzan's fostered an attitude of "why me?" Boy, life was not turning out fine. Instead of strengthening my faith like events did with Suzan, I slid into depression and self-pity.

The next few years are a blur and I still haven't fully "unpacked" everything yet. But, now I was really mad at God. I attended grief counseling classes with a Christian psychologist and read books given me by friends. But now I became angry at everybody else who were just trying as best they knew to help me. All I wanted was for someone to rescue me and do it right away. Well, no one came to rescue me. God was there all along, but I didn't want to listen to Him. So I went on "shopping therapy." I bought stuff I didn't need and couldn't use for an end result of large credit card debt.

Still Stuck on Lucky

I did try dating again without success until I met a woman that my brothers-in-law had hired to be director of sales for ZZC. Tracey was beautiful, confident, and competent. We hit it off and she accepted my proposal in 1999. There were a few rough years financially until 2003 when, quite by accident, I had a casual conversation with a friend at church. We both had daughters in a Sunday school class for special needs kids and I happened to mention I had worked with Zig Ziglar. I don't remember my friend's name but he excitedly said he had a connection with a company and friend who was looking to hire someone with my experience.

After one interview at the D/FW airport, I flew to San Diego to visit with the owner of the company which was of a very similar nature to Zig's company. I got the job and commuted to Atlanta for three months every week until we sold my house and moved the family to Cumming, Georgia.

But again, I was not talking to God. I was still angry, and probably depressed, but I thought I was getting lucky again, I was being rescued. The job only lasted nine months, due to the fact I really wasn't the right guy for the job. I had no working experience outside of a family business and just didn't get it. Again, I was surrounded by outstanding people in a great environment but couldn't get out of my own way, out of my head.

I went to professional counseling (not Christ-based), took antidepressants which had no effect, and got a part-time job with an office supply retailer just to get out of the house. The loss of substantial income caused the loss of our home, serious marital issues, and a period of just giving up.

I did start to get involved with several ministries in the Atlanta area and one in particular, Ministry Ventures. It was an "incubator" for ministry and non-profit organizations by giving them office space and training in starting and operating non-profit organizations. I consulted with several, one in particular called Brave Hearts, an organization that dealt with the issue of pornography and recovery, led by author and speaker Michael Leahy. I helped other organizations as a business consultant writing business plans and serving on the board of a large Christian men's group called Men Step Up led by Kelly Talamo. All this time I was still dealing with depression and feelings of inadequacy.

My mom and dad had moved with us to Georgia from Texas, as had Tracey's mom and dad from Hawaii. As all of their health began to fail, I began to care for them as my work schedule in retail was flexible. I worked the afternoon and evening shifts for five years so I could care for them. Long story short, I saw them all through the end-of-life experience and after they were gone we decided to move back to Texas. Tracey's children had married or moved out on their own and really didn't need us anymore. So, back to Texas we went. I still worked in retail, hated it most of the time, but it was easy work and a good place to "hide out."

We rented for two years or so then bought a house. But my relationship with Tracey deteriorated and reached the lowest point in 2019, when she told me we were selling the house and separating. I was told she had had all she could take of a non-existent relationship with me and no amount of counseling would fix me or our marriage, in her view. Total shock is all I could feel at that moment. I was so sure that nothing like this could happen to me. But in all honesty, I knew exactly at that moment why life had reached this point. I was just in denial, and I knew it.

I did it my way…and look what I got.

I had withdrawn from our relationship into my head, putting on a false front, and I knew we had reached the point of no return. No one was going to rescue me because I wasn't speaking to the only One Who could rescue me, God. I had "delegated" prayer and personal relationships with God to first Suzan and then Tracey. I was trying all these years to manage on my own when the power of the Creator of the universe was waiting for me to just cry out "help." I think the theme song for most of my life up to then really must have been "My Way," the old Frank Sinatra theme song. I can imagine God saying to me, if I had been listening to Him, "How did that work out for you, Chad?" Try doing life all on your own, in your own way, and I can tell you what you'll get and you won't like it.

> I was trying all these years to manage on my own when the power of the Creator of the universe was waiting for me to just cry out "help."

Chapter Five
REWIRING A BRAIN

God: "What say you and I have a moment?"
(Hutch Mansell, the movie *Nobody*, 2021)

Nobody is one of my favorite movies because of the unique combination of action and humor. One scene in which Hutch goes to the villain's nightclub to have a "sit down" about saying "let bygones be bygones" is especially poignant for me. Well, let's just say that God was telling me that now was the "moment of moments" for me and it was time for the reckoning or, as many have said, time for a "come to Jesus" moment. And I made the smartest but most difficult decision I have had to make in my long life. I looked in the

> **And I made the smartest but most difficult decision I have had to make in my long life. I looked in the mirror, saw a very sad man, and told that man, "You are going to have to change everything in your life – the way you think, the way you perceive the world, the way you act, and the way you respond to life – just plain everything."**

mirror, saw a very sad man, and told that man, "You are going to have to change everything in your life – the way you think, the way you perceive the world, the way you act, and the way you respond to life – just plain everything." My thoughts at that moment were, *my life depends on monumental change*. I had to shed one skin and get comfortable in another.

Rewiring a Brain (Yes, It can be done)

Now that sad, sad man did two things that may seem like they came out of nowhere. I committed to making my bed every morning and building a budget spreadsheet to keep track of expenses day to day. These two actions seem random, but to me they were the first concrete steps in becoming accountable. Both were things that forced me to be accountable to ...me. I had to begin change by becoming accountable to myself, to stop lying to myself and start liking myself.

May passed into June and then July. At the fireworks for the Fourth of July celebration in Frisco, Katherine asked me if I had found a counselor yet. I had said that I was going to do that but somehow had not gotten around to it. I think I had at least searched the Internet for Christian psychologists and found a few, but not gotten an appointment yet. Kate raised an eyebrow, and I said I had a name and would call the next day, which I did. I got an appointment the next week with Jonathan. He had a master's degree and was working with and under a licensed therapist, but several months away from being fully licensed. I began weekly appointments and we hit it off well. Well, I say "well" because we had pleasant conversations, but I knew I was not peeling the onion back very far or very fast. It was still all about not revealing my true self to anyone.

Then in December Jonathan told me he couldn't continue working with me as his job situation had changed and he no longer had a licensed therapist to work with. He recommended a biblical counselor whom he knew and respected to continue my journey. I texted Eric Atherton and got an appointment the second week in January. That week in January turned out to be quite a pivotal moment in my journey to reality.

Jumping back to August, three months after hitting the brick wall, separating from Tracey, and picking myself up off the floor after the 2x4 hit me, I had signed up for a program through church called "Rooted." It was advertised as a ten-week program to bring you to a closer relationship to God and learn the rhythms of the Christian life. That sounded to me like a great place to start. I still wasn't attending church every week. I was working in retail and only got one weekend off each month. This program sounded like exactly what I needed to begin a new way of life. It's kind of exciting to know you can start over at any time, isn't it? Well, you can. Everyone can, and it can start right now!

So, there I was, at one particular moment in January 2020, with the opportunity to start with a new counselor and begin an intensive program to reconnect me with God. I really did feel like I was at the edge of a cliff and preparing to jump off. I could die or I could live. I truly believed that if I did not radically change me I would die, but jumping off the cliff offered me a chance to live if I embraced change. I chose to jump for the chance to live.

I had signed up for the "Rooted" program in August, but when I received the first email inviting me to register for the fall session I chickened out and did not register. But in that second week in January I received another email inviting me to register for the spring session. I vividly remember having my hand on my computer mouse with my index finger poised over the left button on the mouse, hesitating out of fear again. I remember the thought in my mind was that my life could depend on what I did in that next instant. Then I felt (really!) a nudge in the middle of my back and my finger twitched and hit the button. I was registered. I was committed.

That same week I had my first meeting with my biblical counselor, Eric Atherton. I can only say that I was an open container of gasoline and Eric brought the match. It was off to the races and there would be no turning back. I immediately decided I had to get down to business with no hiding or retreating from the truth. I would have to be open, transparent, genuine and honest about everything as it all came out: the good, the bad, and the ugly. I confessed everything.

I slinked into that first "Rooted" meeting on Tuesday evening with fear and trepidation, but still committed to genuinely participating and giving my all to the process and the other men in the group. Seven other men of various ages were there; the group leader was Paul, one of the senior pastors at church. They told me later that I crept in wearing a trench coat and with a look on my face between suspicion and fear.

Having biblical counseling and "Rooted" run concurrently was great. It was somewhat like boot camp all over again, but without anyone yelling at me. I was getting a monstrous infusion of God's Word every week. And the icing on the cake was that I was not just sitting and listening to a lecture or reading a book, I was actually building true relationships by being open, transparent, and genuine. Who'd a thunk it? There I was, actually relating to people without a mask on my emotions and thoughts. My actions weren't filtered through a screen of "what would people think?" or "what image am I portraying?" I didn't care what these guys thought as long as I was honest, open, and just real.

Week six in "Rooted" is when we began to give our testimonies. I worked hard on it for a week and finally had what I thought was an honest and genuine testimony. We were given 15 minutes to speak, but I'm sure I went over my limit. No one seemed to mind. I guess my testimony revealed a "colorful" life, more colorful than anyone else in the room. I would later realize that my life was more "colorful" than most of my fellow Preston Trail members. I think l have several more books in me based on some of my experiences.

The revelation here is that when you are open, honest, and transparent, you can live life to its fullest. You have no hidden thoughts as you are relating to others. You don't have to remember what lies you may be telling to preserve an image. The point being that when you exaggerate and tell untruths about yourself and your experience, you have to remember what you told someone and to whom you told it. That behavior will clog up your mind with garbage when the world feeds us more than we can handle as it is. Tell the truth always is the only right thing to do. Do not exaggerate your experiences; the real you is all anyone really wants, that is, anyone who is truly a genuine person themselves.

Too Soon Old and Too Late Smart (old Pennsylvania Dutch saying told me by Dad)

I am now seventy-five and only in the past five years have I realized what I have done, heard, seen, and learned in my life that I now have to share with others. However, not to leave you thinking I'm sad I didn't "get smart" sooner, I want you to know that I am excited that I see it now, finally. Perhaps it has taken so "long to season" and I'm now "ripe" to harvest all the knowledge that now translates into wisdom (hopefully). Well, maybe not all my experiences translate into wisdom I can share, but rather I can teach from them. Some of those not-so-stellar episodes are things not to do. Maybe it all does become wisdom in some ways. But there are some things that my daughter has forbidden me to tell my grandson and I agreed that was probably smart, for now, anyway, as he is only nine years old.

Wisdom comes in many different forms. I have heard my grandson make some very profound statements and I have heard wise perspectives from some who have lived longer than I. I believe that wisdom comes at different times and in different situations. It is up to us as individuals to discern what is wise and what is foolish. Then, it is important that we pass it on.

Wisdom will come as we become aware of our divine purpose and place in God's Kingdom. Each of us is valuable and essential to every other member of the body of Christ. The body cannot function effectively or efficiently without all of us employing the unique gifts we each have been given by the Creator. The Creator created each of us and gave each of us unique gifts to use, to employ and deploy for the benefit of the rest of the body of the church. Make no mistake, every one of us has been given gifts and the purpose is not to sit on them but to use them to reach out to our neighbors. In doing so we display God's love for others, and when they see God's love being displayed and employed, they may welcome God into their hearts.

> **All of human existence, human history has revolved around a search for meaning: why were we created and what are we supposed to do? It is in our "DNA" to seek God. He made us in His own image and seeks to have a relationship with us.**

All of human existence, human history has revolved around a search for meaning: why were we created and what are we supposed to do? It is in our "DNA" to seek God. He made us in His own image and seeks to have a relationship with us.

Jesus left us with instructions with the two greatest commandments: *Jesus replied, "The most important commandment is this: 'Listen, O Israel! The LORD our God is the one and only LORD. And you must love the LORD your God with all your heart, all your soul, all your mind, and all your strength.' The second is equally important: 'Love your neighbor as yourself.' No other commandment is greater than these."* (Mark 12:29-31 NLT)

Why does Satan want to distract us? He was given temporary dominion over the world (until the return of Jesus). He thinks that he can win the war against God. Satan seeks to kill and devour, according to Scripture. Satan's best tools in his toolbox are distractions. Distractions are the easiest for Satan to use because we facilitate and embrace distractions. We are our own worst enemies. And, sadly, I can include all of us in that crowd.

> *"Indeed the safest road to hell is the gradual one – the gentle slope, soft underfoot without sudden turnings, without milestones, without signposts."(Screwtape Letters,* C.S. Lewis)

Isolation is Satan's most valuable and useful tool, especially for men. When we are isolated mentally, emotionally, and physically, he can attack and devour us. We are at our weakest when we isolate ourselves. I don't mean when we are praying or fasting, studying or reading, but when we withdraw into ourselves, separating from relationships and, most specifically, from community with other believers.

> *Stay alert! Watch out for your great enemy, the devil. He prowls around like a roaring lion, looking for someone to devour. Stand firm against him, and be strong in your faith. Remember that your family of believers all over the world is going through the same kind of suffering you are.*(1 Peter 5:8-11, NLT)

Envy: *"It's not greed that drives the world, but envy." The idea of caring is that someone is making money faster [than you are] is one of the deadly sins. What good is envy? It's the one sin you can't have any fun at. Envy is a really stupid sin because it's the only one you could never possibly have any fun at. There's a lot of pain and no fun. Why would you want to get on that trolley?"* (Charlie Munger, Warren Buffet's partner)

The definition of affluence: money, success, possessions as in a plentiful supply of material goods, a great quantity, an abundance, wealth.

I found an antidote to envy and I'll tell you where I found it. I didn't find it in Scripture, although it is written there in many places. I found it in a book we used in our morning men's group, *Life Without Lack* by Dallas Willard. I learned it can be achieved only by "dying to self," a principle of stop thinking about your own needs and desires and trusting that God already has a plan for your life and if you will trust Him, you will experience the abundant life He promises.

It's not easy to "die to self." It's especially hard in the affluent world we live in here in America, the so-called "western world." It takes time and effort to rewire our thinking to embrace the concept of "dying to self." I know it did me.

Principle of Inversion

Munger is famous for his quote, *"All I want to know is where I'm going to die, so I'll never go there."* This thinking, according to Charlie, was inspired by the German mathematician Carl Jacobi, who often solved difficult problems by following a simple strategy: *man muss immerumkehren* (or loosely translated, "invert, always invert"). "[Jacobi] knew that it is in the nature of things that many hard problems are best solved when they are addressed backward," Munger counsels. "Indeed, many problems can't be solved forward."

> *"If you don't learn to constantly revise your earlier conclusions, and get better ones...you're like a one-legged man in an ass-kicking contest."* Charles Munger

My take on Charlie's quotes is that if you are not getting the results in life you expect or want, think backwards from a new goal, the abundant life God has promised. It is hard, if not impossible, to change little things you are doing, habits, behaviors, and what-not. These things are especially hard to change in the short term. But, if you will realign your ultimate life goal, all the things in the way, the distractions, will be easier to change and some will just fall into place.

What have you got to lose?

Chapter Six
DISTRACTIONS CAN KILL

Now to the crux of the matter: The distractions, idols, and the other cxxp that were killing me.

I realized four-and-a-half years ago when God finally got my full, undivided attention, that I was anxious and fearful of nearly everything and everybody. I became very anxious when I read anything about national news, politics, what was happening anywhere in the world, and fearful of how it could impact me. Everything was a distraction from the real point of life.

I had now identified where to look, Who to look to, and what I had to begin doing and thinking. But the distractions were everywhere. There was the Internet, television, sports, international conflicts, drugs, cartels, the border, mean people, the other political party, people who didn't believe what I believed or hold my values to be true and, of course, the economy. Literally everything outside of my head and little apartment distracted me, caused anxiety, and scared the dickens out of me.

What's the point if we are so distracted by everything in the world and our lives that we don't have time for, and we can't see, the truly important things in this life? The point is that we have to recognize and make decisions regarding what we allow into our lives on a daily, even hourly basis.

Admittedly, my being retired should make it easier to identify and manage the distractions in my life. That does not mean I am immune to any of the effects of distractions and having to decide what's important and what can be managed or eliminated. I am still bombarded every day by the distractions of modern, everyday life. The temptation to follow distractions and waste time, effort, and resources is to the detriment of what is truly important in my life. If you make a commitment to follow Jesus and building the Kingdom, the distractions the enemy will throw at you will increase and become more dangerous.

The biggest distraction beginning in the twentieth century and accelerating rapidly in the twenty-first century, the World Wide Web (www), or the Internet as we now call it, is unarguably the most wonderful creation of modern times – yet the most invasive and destructive invention at the same time.

I don't have to say much more than the creators of our digital world have said and continue to say. I apologize for reprinting long articles from the Internet, but what is said is important and needs to be emphasized.

The Internet Apologizes ... (I was right, for once!)

I have always been uncomfortable with the intrusive nature of the Internet and the condition of being always connected to it day and night, wherever you go. I have always felt that someone was looking over my shoulder and prying into my personal affairs (and I was right). I was late to relent and get a smartphone and a personal computer. I even resisted having a pc installed in my office. My excuse for that was, "If I need a report or any information, I'll ask you to get it for me because that's what I hired you for…"

Even those who designed our digital world are aghast at what they created. A breakdown of what went wrong — from the architects who built it.

"I Was Devastated": Tim Berners-Lee, the man who created the World Wide Web, has some regrets.

Something has gone wrong with the Internet. Even Mark Zuckerberg knows it. Testifying before congress, the Facebook CEO ticked off a list of everything his platform has screwed up, from fake news and foreign meddling in the 2016 election to hate speech and data privacy. "We didn't take a broad enough view of our responsibility," he confessed. Then he added the words that everyone was waiting for: "I'm sorry."

Cell Phones, a Blessing and a Curse

The man who oversaw the creation of the original iPhone believes the device he helped build is too addictive. The inventor of the World Wide Web fears his creation is being "weaponized." Even Sean Parker, Facebook's first president, has blasted social media as a dangerous form of psychological manipulation. *"God only knows what it's doing to our children's brains,"* he lamented recently. (Noah Kulwin, *The Intelligencer*)

Look at all the Internet has added to our lives. Instant news, everything said, written, or recorded by a person since forever, pornography, hate speech, instant notoriety for terrorists and violent criminals, front row seats for wars, catastrophes, adulterous hookups, scams. Then, on the flip side, you have the sum total of man's knowledge, Wikipedia for example, and just about anything you want to know, not to say everything you wanted to know from doctors but they don't tell you.

It used to be that with down time we would read a book, write a letter, have a conversation or just relax. Now we fill every moment with screen time. We can't spend a moment not being entertained. People walk the streets with eyes fastened to little bitty screens instead of looking where they are going or just enjoying the view.

> It used to be that with down time we would read a book, write a letter, have a conversation or just relax. Now we fill every moment with screen time. We can't spend a moment not being entertained.

I still get a lot of static from my family, mainly my daughter, when I forget to carry my phone with me. If she calls me and I don't answer, she might send my son-in-law in his car over to find out if I'm ok. That just annoys him and results in a lecture I want to avoid from everybody.

Now Artificial Intelligence is the Latest Scare from Technology and the Internet

Remember the movies *The Matrix* and *Terminator*? In case you were sleeping or just in a coma, *The Matrix* is a 1999 science fiction action film depicting a dystopian future in which humanity is unknowingly trapped inside the Matrix, a simulated reality that intelligence machines have created to distract humans while using their bodies as an energy source. There have been three sequels to the original, the latest released in 2021.

Terminator is a 1984 American science fiction action film that depicts the Terminator, a cyborg assassin sent back in time from 2029 to 1984 to kill Sarah Connor, whose unborn son will one day save mankind from extinction by Skynet, a hostile *artificial intelligence* in a post-apocalyptic future. Terminator has seen five sequels concluding in 2019 (and more to come, I understand).

Both movies and their sequels were built around scenarios that have now been duplicated in reality in the present time.The Meta-verse invites you in and you end up spending enormous amounts of time and money staying there. Or, are we really just trapped in a pseudo-reality as depicted in *The Matrix*? Never mind.

When those movies first came out we thought it represented a distant future that foretold the theoretical and potential demise of the human race. It was just science fiction about a reality that could never become real, right? Well, guess what? The future is here. Not just the Internet. That's considered just child's play now. The real scary future has come to us at light speed and is changing our lives now, not some time in the future.

The *"Father of AI is Scared."* (Excerpted from BBC article)

A man widely seen as the "godfather" of artificial intelligence (AI) has quit his job, warning about the growing dangers from developments in the field. Even he is scared for the future if AI is not restrained and safeguards built in.

Geoffrey Hinton, 75, announced his resignation from Google in a statement to the New York Times, saying he now regretted his work. He told the BBC some of the dangers of AI chatbots were "quite scary. Right now, they're not more intelligent than us, as far as I can tell. But I think they soon may be. There's an enormous upside from this technology, but it's essential that the world invests heavily and urgently in AI safety and control," he said.

Dr. Hinton also told the BBC that "in the shorter term" he thought AI would deliver many more benefits than risks, "so I don't think we should stop developing this stuff," he added. But Dr. Hinton joins a growing number of experts who have expressed concerns about AI - both the speed at which it is developing and the direction in which it is going.

"We Need to Take a Step Back"

In March, an open letter - co-signed by dozens of people in the AI field - including the tech billionaire Elon Musk - called for a pause on all developments more advanced than the current version of AI chatbot, ChatGPT, so robust safety measures could be designed and implemented.

Yoshua Bengio, another so-called "godfather" of AI, who along with Dr. Hinton and Yann LeCun won the 2018 Turing Award for their work on deep learning, also signed the letter. Mr. Bengio wrote that it was because of the "unexpected acceleration" in AI systems that "we need to take a step back."

He also said that international competition would mean that a pause would be difficult. "Even if everybody in the US stopped developing it, China would just get a big lead," he said.

Dr. Hinton also said he was an expert on the science, not policy, and that it was the responsibility of government to ensure AI was developed "with a lot of thought into how to stop it going rogue."

"Responsible Approach"

Dr. Hinton stressed that he did not want to criticize Google and that the tech giant had been "very responsible." "I actually want to say some good things about Google. And they're more credible if I don't work for Google."

In a statement, Google's chief scientist Jeff Dean said: "We remain committed to a responsible approach to AI. We're continually learning to understand emerging risks while also innovating boldly."

It is important to remember that AI chatbots are just one aspect of artificial intelligence, even if they are the most popular right now.

AI is behind the algorithms that dictate what video-streaming platforms decide you should watch next. It can be used in recruitment to filter job applications, by insurers to calculate premiums, it can diagnose medical conditions (although human doctors still get the final say).

> *What we are seeing now though is the rise of AGI - artificial general intelligence - which can be trained to do a number of things within a remit. So, for example, ChatGPT can only offer text answers to a query, but the possibilities within that, as we are seeing, are endless.*
>
> *But the pace of AI acceleration has surprised even its creators. It has evolved dramatically since Dr. Hinton built a pioneering image analysis neural network in 2012.*
>
> *Even Google boss Sundar Pichai said in a recent interview that even he did not fully understand everything that its AI chatbot, Bard, did.*
>
> *Make no mistake, we are on a speeding train right now, and the concern is that one day it will start building its own tracks.*(By Zoe Kleinman & Chris Vallance BBC News May 2, 2023)

The whole objective of AI, in my opinion, is to simulate an intelligence that exceeds the human intellect and approach a God-like state of consciousness. Not a worthwhile endeavor, even considering the medical advancements that AI potentially could provide. Look what happened to nuclear power without safeguards and guidelines in place before it all got out of hand.

Again, I apologize for reprinting long passages from Internet articles, but I want to be certain I accurately reproduce the thoughts and words of the individuals quoted. I am not an expert in the digital sciences and I feel it is important to be accurate when I am pointing out the dangers we face.

My conclusion of all this is that mankind is trying to create a perfect world without disease, war, bias, mimicking the Garden of Eden as a way of claiming the throne from God.

Politics was a huge source of anxiety for me. I tied my emotions to the party, candidates, and issues that fit my predilections (my personal likes, dislikes, values and hot buttons), and my state of mind ebbed and flowed according to who was saying the right things this week, appearing to get the upper hand in debates, or was espousing more of the values (or close to them) that I thought I believed in. The political landscape was a minefield for me of valleys and mountains. I either was elated or dejected, my enthusiasm rising or falling, and I never felt at peace with anything at any time. I never unpacked all this until the election year of 2020. I was alone, having separated the year earlier, and had begun the process of dissecting my life to figure out why I was such a mess.

One day I came to the conclusion that I was just downright disgusted with everything about the political state of America nationally, statewide, and locally. I was disgusted and fed up with everything, everybody, and everywhere. I was immersing myself in Scripture, really seeking God's plan for my life, and realized that I had spent the majority of my life on the wrong road. I wasn't wrong about everything, but my perspective on everything was distorted. I had raised the issues of life to a level of importance in my life that they didn't deserve. God did not, does not care about 99% of the stuff we obsess over. He is not concerned about whether we care about who is elected president, or governor, mayor, or sheriff. He is in control of all that and we aren't supposed to be frightened or feel anxious about it all.

God only cares about one thing and that is His most important commandment and how we obey it and live by it. *"Love the Lord your God with all your heart, and with all your soul, and with all your mind. This is the first and greatest commandment. And the second is like it: Love your neighbor as yourself. All the Law and the Prophets hang on these two commandments."* (Matt 22:37-40, NIV)

When I put everything into the perspective of that commandment, I realized that our job as Christians and Christian churches is not to get involved in the politics. When we do, with the heightened emotions and angry rhetoric that has evolved today, we alienate the half of our fellow Americans that we are charged with loving, discipling, and leading.

> When I put everything into the perspective of that commandment, I realized that our job as Christians and Christian churches is not to get involved in the politics.

Then I attended the Global Leadership Conference and I listened as Andy Stanley spoke about the same exact issues that had troubled me and eventually led me to a new perspective.

Political Distractions – "Not in it to Win it"

Let's talk about a very divisive issue confronting Christians in America today that is increasingly sidelining the church and creating haters out there.

I attended both days of the 2022 Annual Global Leadership Conference at Preston Trail Community Church, where the conference is a live feed by satellite and has been for several years. Up to last year, I have never been able to take two days off during the week because of my work schedule.

What I learned about at the 2022 GLC only served to reinforce the views and conclusions I had come to believe on my own over the past four years. God gave me the mission and purpose of writing a book that hopefully will lead people, including believers, back to basics and simple truths: the basics that Jesus taught and commanded us to practice if we are to truly follow Him.

God loves us, every one, and commands us to love others as ourselves and as He loves us. And that means everyone. Our purpose as believers is not to convert our nation to a "Christian nation." It is not to be Republican or Democrat, nor is it to love only those who look like us, dress like us, drive cars like us, or live in our neighborhoods. It is not to love only those who live in our country, were born here, make us feel comfortable, or don't scare us because they don't have a home and might live in their car. The list goes on.

I highly recommend Andy Stanley's book, *Not in It to Win It - Why choosing sides sidelines the church*, if you want to rebuild your world-view on principles that created the dynamic growth of "The Way" in the first and second century.

Religion

Just sitting in church will not make you a better Christian any more than sitting in your garage will make you into a car.

God cannot use the gifts He has blessed you with if you don't get out there and practice loving your neighbor. Get involved in your church, community, nation, and world. Your neighbors are everywhere. Your individual gifts are needed somewhere in the world today, right now. Find out where you can help. Type into any Internet search engine "love your neighbor" and see what you get.

> **Your individual gifts are needed somewhere in the world today, right now. Find out where you can help.**

"*A moderated religion is as good for us as no religion at all – and more amusing.*" (*Screwtape Letters*, C.S. Lewis)

"*It does not matter how small the sins are provided that their cumulative effect is to edge the man away from the Light and out into the Nothing. Murder is no better than cards if cards can do the trick. Indeed the safest road to Hell is the gradual one--the gentle slope, soft underfoot, without sudden turnings, without milestones, without signposts.*"(C.S. Lewis)

Are you starting to get the picture?

"*Politicians and diapers must be changed often, and for the same reason.*" (Mark Twain)

"*The church or church leader who publicly aligns with a political party has relinquished their ability to make disciples of half their own nation, much less all nations.*" (Andy Stanley)

Here are a few headlines that illuminate a significant problem with the church in America today.

A group of 25 pastors and faith leaders had an exclusive meeting with the president at the White House Tuesday, Oct. 29. During that meeting, the president reportedly asked the pastors to lay hands on him and pray.

50 pastors call out ministers who met with the president. (13th August 2018) Bishop Paul S. Morton, Sr., spiritual leader of Greater St. Stephen Full Gospel Baptist Church in New Orleans, was among more than 50 African-American pastors who felt compelled to respond after a highly publicized meeting between the president and 20 black ministers that was long on style but short on substance.

After the highly criticized meeting, the group of more than 50 pastors from across the country penned an open letter to those who participated in the meeting, expressing their concern and dissent. In the letter, the 20 pastors are referred to as "presidential cheerleaders" who were used by the president's administration in an effort to dupe black voters into supporting the president and his allies in upcoming elections.

Pastors who prayed with President Trump accused of heresy. Reverend William Barber II brands Oval Office prayer meeting "theological malpractice."

Evangelical Leaders Lay Hands On the President In Group Prayer. President Trump met with Christian leaders in the Oval Office on Monday for a prayer gathering. The practice *isn't new for Trump, who has participated in a number of intimate gatherings with faith leaders during his campaign and into his presidency.*

"Saving America is not the mission of the church. The moment our love or concern for country takes precedence over our love for the people in our country, we are off mission....Again, we lose our elevated position as the conscience of the nation. We give up the moral high ground." (Andy Stanley)

> ***"If voting made any difference, they wouldn't let us do it."*** (Mark Twain)

Now many of you are going to hate on me, but here goes.

America is not a "chosen" nation. It is not a Christian nation. It was not created as a Christian nation and cannot be made over into a Christian nation. There is a small, fringe group of people called Black Robe Regiment who are calling for clergy to take bolder stances in defense of liberty. These guys even supported the January 6th demonstrations at the Capitol. They are preaching a theology that equates Christianity with democracy and that America needs a "make-over."

Strange, because I don't recall reading in my Bible that Jesus Christ ever said his followers should overthrow the Romans or Herod, the king of the Jews. Maybe I can't remember it because it's not there. Jesus did say something like this:

> *Later they sent some of the Pharisees and Herodians to Jesus to catch him in his words. They came to him and said, "Teacher, we know that you are a man of*

> *integrity. You aren't swayed by others, because you pay no attention to who they are; but you teach the way of God in accordance with the truth. Is it right to pay the imperial tax to Caesar or not?*
>
> *"Should we pay or shouldn't we?" But Jesus knew their hypocrisy. "Why are you trying to trap me?" He asked. "Bring me a denarius and let me look at it."*
>
> *They brought the coin, and he asked them, "Whose image is this? And whose inscription?" "Caesar's," they replied.*
>
> *Then Jesus said to them, "Give back to Caesar what is Caesar's and to God what is God's." And they were amazed at him.* (Mark 12:13-17)

And we wonder why more Americans find the Christian church (all denominations included) to be exclusive, bigoted, hateful, and on and on.

> **"The church or church leader who publicly aligns with a political party has relinquished their ability to make disciples of half their own nation, much less all nations."** (Andy Stanley *Not in It to Win It*)

Prosperity Theology

Here is another huge distraction that some in the church have brought on themselves: the theological perspective termed the "Prosperity Gospel." Here is what Wikipedia says about it.

> ***Prosperity theology*** *(sometimes referred to as the* ***prosperity gospel****, the* ***health and wealth gospel****, the* ***gospel of success****, or* ***seed faith****) is a religious belief among some Protestant Christians that financial*

blessing and physical well-being are always the will of God for them, and that faith, positive speech, and donations to religious causes will increase one's material wealth. Material and especially financial success is seen as a sign of divine favor.

Prosperity theology has been criticized by leaders from various Christian denominations, including within some Pentecostal and charismatic movements, who maintain that it is irresponsible, promotes idolatry, and is contrary to the Bible. Secular as well as some Christian observers have also criticized prosperity theology as exploitative of the poor. The practices of some preachers have attracted scandal and some have been charged with financial fraud.

Prosperity theology views the Bible as a contract between God and humans: if humans have faith in God, He will deliver security and prosperity. The doctrine emphasizes the importance of personal empowerment, proposing that it is God's will for His people to be blessed. The atonement (reconciliation with God) is interpreted to include the alleviation of sickness and poverty, which are viewed as curses to be broken by faith. This is believed to be achieved through donations of money, visualization, and positive confession. (Wikipedia)

News Flash

God is not a cosmic vending machine where you can walk up and say, "I want this and I will do this for it," or "I will do this if you will do that." Money,

> **Life becomes so much more peaceful and calm when we seek a "Life Without Lack"**

wealth, power and prosperity are distractions of the most seductive nature.

Life becomes so much more peaceful and calm when we seek a "Life Without Lack," which happens to be a book by Dallas Willard. Seeking, pursuing and achieving a life without lack, with everything you need provided by God in His sufficiency, is truly "heaven on earth."

Chapter Seven

THE CULTURE WAR DISTRACTION

If the point of life is to obey God's two most important commandments as spoken to us by Jesus Christ, then distractions and the culture wars are the tools used by forces in the world (Satan) to hide, conceal, and distract us from knowing, believing, and accomplishing the most important things we can do in our lives and to help others do the same.

I realized, as I was sitting in a darkened, one-bedroom apartment that May 10th in 2019, that I had to change everything I thought, everything I did, and everything that I thought were my values. I think that about covers everything about me that made me a person, a living being. I did not include my physical appearance, although having more hair on the top of my head would not have hurt.

Distractions have been around since Genesis and the Garden of Eden (you know, the beginning of everything – or close to it). Remember the snake? Well he created the first distraction, the Big Lie. Yep, that's when it all started.

The Big Lie was the first distraction. That's when we began to be distracted from our purpose for existing – being in a loving relationship with God.

Here is where I introduce the villain of our story, Satan, the father of lies and the devourer of the faithful. Big title, as befitting a big problem.

In all seriousness, the problem we have is a huge problem. It has presented problems since the beginning and it only gets worse every day. Distractions have always been with us, but today the sheer quantity that we are faced with is staggering. Think of social media, television, the Internet, children, job, traffic, cars, house, possessions, success, parents, money, and the list goes on and on.

> "It does not matter how small the sins are provided that their cumulative effect is to edge the man away from the Light and out into the Nothing. Murder is no better than cards if cards can do the trick. Indeed the safest road to Hell is the gradual one--the gentle slope, soft underfoot, without sudden turnings, without milestones, without signposts."(C.S. Lewis)

Bad Distractions

I think everyone will nod your head and agree that drugs, alcohol, and sex are easy to identify as bad, undesirable, and destructive distractions. Illegal drugs in any form, used to any degree, will destroy users, family, friends, neighborhoods, cities, and nations. The evidence is everywhere every day. Alcohol used to excess to compensate for emotional and psychological issues destroys as well, and the evidence is everywhere. Sex outside of God's given parameters is destructive of relationships, marriages, families, and communities, including churches. Again, the evidence is everywhere.

Distractions never stop; they are everywhere and can be anything that distracts us from our *raisond'être*, our reason for living. In the beginning, in the Garden, our *reason for being* was to love God and take care of the earth and all His creations. Now our reason for living, the point of it all, hasn't changed. It is to love God and love our neighbors as ourselves and take care of the world and all that inhabit it. Simple?

But, that does not suit the villain of our story. He still believes that he can win his war with God and will do anything and everything to keep every soul from believing that God loves us, we are to love God, and we can achieve the abundant life God has promised to those who believe and trust Him.

Forgive me if I seem flippant and perhaps unserious at times, but I'm having the time of my life now. It may have taken many years, too many years, to figure some things out, but I have come to understand why I exist, my *raisond'être, if* you will, and I enjoy every day. So, please indulge me and allow me to continue, stay with me and let's get back to the distractions of life. First we will identify some, but not all, because there are far too many and new ones are created every day, even while we sleep.

Render unto Caesar...

> *"Tell us then, what is your opinion? Is it right to pay the imperial tax to Caesar or not?" But Jesus, knowing their evil intent, said, "You hypocrites, why are you trying to trap me? Show me the coin used for*

> *paying the tax." They brought him a denarius, and he asked them, "Whose image is this? And whose inscription?"*
>
> *"Caesar's," they replied. Then he said to them, "So give back to Caesar what is Caesar's, and to God what is God's." When they heard this, they were amazed. So they left him and went away.* (Matthew 22:17-22)

Did Jesus allow Himself to get embroiled in the culture wars of His time? No, He did not. Should we become obsessed with the culture wars of today? We should not to the point where we are distracted from God's prime directive. The incredible growth of the church in the first and second centuries was possible because the Christians did not challenge the societies and the rulers of societies. Instead, they lived their lives differently. For instance, instead of challenging the norm of discarding female and imperfect newborn babies, they simply rescued them from the trash heaps and raised them as their own. Think about how far they would have gotten if they had demonstrated against that practice and challenged authority. Not far, probably gotten themselves jailed or worse, executed by crucifixion.

How have the culture wars affected me and my relationships? I look back on my life up to recently and can see clearly how what was going on in the world, in my country, my state and city, filled up my waking hours and produced anxiety, worry, fear, anger and hatred. It filled my mind. I spent so much time thinking about all this that I began to withdraw into my own head a long time ago. I felt I had to contain my thoughts because they were too scary to share with anyone else. I feared how others would react to my thoughts if I revealed them. So, the mask went up and became more encompassing as time passed.

The shell hardened to a point where I did not even realize what was happening to me. I lost touch with family and the few friends I had at the time.

Don't Get Caught up in Culture Wars

How can we win disciples for Christ when we alienate anyone and everyone we don't agree with?

Stop. We can't forget that we live in the world and the world is ruled by Satan, for a while. We can become so absorbed in contesting and winning every confrontation with the ways of the world that we forget that we can't remake the whole world into the image of what the Kingdom should look like here on earth. Christ did not try to change the Roman Empire and we should not expect to change the world around us. We can vote and advocate for everything as we are doing now, but do not think for a minute that God expects us to change the whole world into His Kingdom here on earth as it is in heaven. That comes later.

The first and second century church grew at a phenomenal rate because they lived and acted as Jesus commanded, not because they tried to change the world around them politically. God wants us to change one person at a time. Jesus changed hearts, not nations.

I was nearing completion on the first draft of this book when, early on a Saturday morning while I waited for my car wash to be completed, I had this thought. Actually I had woken up with this thought, as many of the thoughts of what I write come to me as I am waking up. I wake with a thought dominating my mind and I have to write it down quickly as I tend to forget it if I don't do it soon. This is it.

The news, whether on television, the Internet news like CNN, Fox News, Newsmax, or a hundred other news sites, liberal, conservative or "neutral" (unbiased, if that could be), what do you see?

You will see stories that bolster your worldviews or undercut your belief according to how you see the world. If the stories support or confirm your perspectives you feel justified, or good, that someone thinks like you or is championing the "correct" views. You like that and feel comfortable, and if everyone thought like you and that person the world would be a better place.

If what you see and read is contrary to your views, it infuriates you, attacks you, and threatens you and your family. You become angry and the human tendency is to reject, fear, even hate the viewpoints, opinions, and circumstances you are viewing.

Then your feelings are transferred to the people in the stories whose opinions, viewpoints, perspectives, and beliefs are described. Anxiety turns to fear and fear becomes, too often, hate.

So now the question becomes: *In view of the Lord's commandments in Matthew 22: 37-40, love your God and second, love your neighbor as yourself, how can you love your neighbors (that's everybody except you) if you hate them, if their beliefs anger you, their behavior disgusts you? How do you love someone when every word out of their mouth creates fear, anxiety, and loathing? How do you love the people who want to kill you, your family, your friends, or your way of life?* It's not easy.

The people who are the object of your fear, anxiety, and anger are your neighbors, who we are commanded to love. If you are a believer, and I believe all who profess that Jesus is your Lord and Savior truly have the best intentions at heart, how do you, how do we overcome our sinful nature that creates all these feelings in us?

I have them, everybody has them. The challenge we all have, the overarching desire of God for us, is to rise above our sinful nature as a new creature and in our re-born state fully embrace His commands, reach out and truly love everyone.

Some can, some won't, and the rest of us struggle every day to follow God's desires for us and His commandments.

Life is simple. God's plan follows the principle of K.I.S.S., but when people try to walk the walk, our feet become entangled by our sinful nature with a strong assist from Satan, the simplest form being the many distractions we face in today's world.

What's at Stake? What Happens if You Don't?

Hypocrisy

Spending time, effort, and resources on "Image Management" has been an issue with humankind since, well, the beginning of time, creation. Image management occurs at every level of societies from pauper to king. Spending time, effort, and resources on managing one's image rather than developing one's character is self-defeating at best, and destructive at worst, for you and everybody around you.

Image management can also be viewed as concealing the real you. It is living with the intention of presenting a false representation of who you really are. It develops a lack of transparency, dishonesty, disingenuousness, lies, and obfuscations. Are you getting a picture of what that person looks like? It promotes an effort "to be all things to all people." First of all, it can't be done. No one can be all things to all people without being at the same time fake.

> Image management can also be viewed as concealing the real you. It is living with the intention of presenting a false representation of who you really are.

Success: If you are success-driven, channel that zeal into becoming the best at "neighboring." The first century church did that and changed the world. They didn't get involved in issues with the Roman Empire, with the Pharisees or Sadducees, or the governments of the day or social issues of the time. They focused on living every day as Jesus did.

Wealth: the drive for wealth in and of itself is not worthwhile.

> *"For the love of money is a root of all kinds of evil. Some people, eager for money, have wandered from the faith and pierced themselves with many griefs."*
> (1 Timothy 6:10 NIV)

Wealth and striving for success should be viewed as a function of the desire to do more to "love your neighbors." How can we use our blessings to love our neighbors?

Possessions:

Cars, homes, clothes, vacations and lifestyle, are all well and good but not as a destination. "I'll be happy when I get a new car, house, or suit." No, you won't. God gives you what you need, when you need it, if you are focused on Him and His mission for you in your life. A new suit never made me a better man, it just made me think it did, so I bought plenty – and shoes to go with them. I spent so much time, effort, and money on building and maintaining my image that I neglected to consider my character. Sad.

Busyness:

The busyness of life shows how we can fill our lives with so many distractions and stuff, thinking it's all important and leaving no time for our spiritual edification. We are not mere physical beings, rather we are spiritual beings. We were created in our God's own image and imbued with a spirit that will endure after the physical aspect of our being is no more.

There is no such thing as "busyness." It is actually a series or the culmination of the small choices and little decisions we make every day. We make hundreds of small decisions

Kids:

Having kids is not an issue. Even having multiple kids is not a problem (make sure you are asking God for direction before you continue doing what you're doing). But it is how you raise children and align with your mission and purpose within God's will for your life.

Multiple kids involved with multiple activities, including sports, leaves little time for mental, emotional, and spiritual development or time for really important things. No, your kid probably will never become a rich professional athlete who can support you, but I think many parents may have that in the back of their mind. If it is the child's dream and desire, that's one thing and they should pursue it until it is no longer an option. But, they might have to choose one, not three or four.

The challenge for parents is that too many activities leave little time for important things like spiritual, mental, and emotional development. Think and plan very carefully if you have several children. They all can't, probably shouldn't, do more than one sport per season per child. My grandson, at eight, sometimes has three sports overlapping.

> **Do not fall into the trap of allowing children to be an excuse for not taking time to grow spiritually as an adult.**

But here's a kicker: Do not fall into the trap of allowing children to be an excuse for not taking time to grow spiritually as an adult. I hear and see a lot of parents using their children's school, athletics, friends, vacations, and shopping as reasons they can't spend time in volunteering and groups at church, retreats, marriage conferences, and many other activities that would build strong relationships, marriages, and families.

Children are important, make no mistake. But growing and maturing as a follower of Jesus is really more important than some of the time and activities that children demand. Balance is key, as is a long view of what is most vital to a family's well-being and the health of the relationship of the parents. If the parents don't have a healthy relationship on all levels, it will negatively affect the family dynamics and the emotional development of the children.

So, is it more important to spend an hour each week running the kids to one more athletic event, school, friends, or activity than spend one hour in growing spiritually yourself in order to maintain a healthy environment for the whole family into the future? You make the call.

Think about the times you took an airplane anywhere. Remember the cabin crew explaining the emergency procedures? Every airplane trip anywhere, anytime, these instructions were carefully explained to all passengers. When explaining what would happen if the cabin became de-pressurized, the oxygen masks would fall down from the overhead. What was the next instruction? Yes, it was if you were traveling with children, put your own mask on first. Do not put the child's mask on first, put your own mask on first, then you can help the child by putting their mask on.

Why? Because you cannot help the child if you pass out due to lack of oxygen. Your health and survival is essential to the health and survival of the child. The very same logic can be applied to the family, every family. If Mom and Dad do not have a healthy relationship and a growing maturity in their spiritual life, then the family will not be healthy and the children will not have the best chance of growing up into mature and emotionally healthy adults. It's all about the journey.

Can children grow up into mature and emotionally healthy adults without parents who are growing relationally and spiritually? Yes, they can, because God is really in charge at the end of the day. Today we have a lot of one-parent families, blended families, and dysfunctional families, but it doesn't always have to be that way.

My own story is one of "checking the box." Even after accepting Jesus as my Lord and Savior, I abdicated the praying and spiritual growth activities to someone else. It was either my wife or a more devout family member. I apparently assumed that living in the same house, sitting in church, or being part of a Godly family gave me a pass on doing the work myself. I was not growing spiritually or closer into a meaningful relationship with God.

Additionally, I will also add a very important aspect of a balanced life, especially for men. Men require community. Way back in time, a man would probably be a warrior and he had a lot of men around him. Now it is too common and way too easy for men to become isolated. Isolation for men can often be deadly: deadly emotionally, spiritually, and health-wise. The first two are critical. When men are isolated without "comrades" or running buddies, they turn to living inside their head. I did.

What it produces is a withdrawal from relationships, with your spouse, if not married then with your significant other, or with friends and groups. Women do pretty well, for the most part, with having friends and groups to connect with. Men, on the other hand, do not. Men who want to grow spiritually and emotionally, men who desire to seek wisdom, must have community. They must have an environment where they can be open, transparent, and honest without judgment and with unconditional acceptance.

Where are you going to get that in the world in which we live? The best place to look is church, filled with other believers who are looking for the same thing you are. If your church does not have an environment that allows or fosters that, get out and find a community that does. They are out there.

In retrospect, it all makes sense because I was "doing it my way." The journey was difficult, the results were not great, and people were hurt in the process. All needlessly, I will add.

So, deciding to make the investment now in your relationship with God, spiritual growth and maturity, the relationship between you and your spouse and balanced family relationships, makes all kinds of sense to me.

> **We all want as parents to provide all our children with the opportunities to find what they are good at and have fun doing it. But finding a balance between children's needs and your needs is challenging.**

We all want as parents to provide all our children with the opportunities to find what they are good at and have fun doing it. But finding a balance between children's needs and your needs is challenging. Remember the airplane and make a huge effort to attend to the well-being and spiritual growth of the two most important people in the family.

Well, enough meddling on my part (for the time being anyway). I'll leave you with this:

> *"Indeed the safest road to hell is the gradual one – the gentle slope, soft underfoot without sudden turnings, without milestones, without signposts."*
> (Again, another scary thought.) (C.S. Lewis)

Chapter Eight
WHAT DO YOU HAVE TO LOSE?

I had lived my life one way up to the ripe old age of 70 when I was faced with the reality that nothing was working as planned. "Doing me" had led to being alone, without a house for a home, a failed marriage, and facing a dark, dismal future. I did make two important decisions that first day I was alone. I decided if I accomplished nothing else, I would at least make my bed every day so I could say I finished one task. The next thing I decided I must do was to change how I approached everything and everything I thought was true about myself. I know I have said this before but it's worth repeating again. Write a book.

What Do You Have to Gain or Lose?

Nothing! Take an inventory of your life today and is it everything you would hope for, everything you planned? Nobody's life has turned out the way they imagined when young, when they graduated from high school, college, got married, had

> **Nobody can plan and live a perfect life.**

children, or whenever they sat down to dream or set goals. Nobody can plan and live a perfect life.

Changing the Engines on the Plane While in Flight

Now the fun begins. I spent some time in the U.S. Air Force during the Vietnam Era, as it's called now. I lived on air bases for almost four years and learned a lot about what it takes to keep our Air Force in the air. When you look up and see an airplane flying effortlessly across the sky, you have no idea what it takes to get there unless you've been "behind the scenes." One statistic I found says that every hour of flight time for a Boeing C-17 Globemaster transport aircraft requires 20 man hours of maintenance time. Another stat says that Air Force tankers require 30 to 40 hours of maintenance for every hour of flight time. The B-2 bomber requires over 100 hours of maintenance for every hour of flight (after all, it has been over 70 years since its first flight in 1952).

Whatever the figure, it doesn't matter. If you have to change the engine on a plane, is it easier to change the engine while the plane is on the ground or when it is in the air? Silly, but apply this thinking to life, your life. If you wait until a crisis appears – and it will, as it does in every life – you are less likely to make or be able to make dramatic changes in the middle of a crisis. You are far more involved in damage control and avoiding more disaster.

Prepare Before Taking Off

Time spent in maintenance, on the ground, is time spent in growing spiritually, emotionally, and physically. Building a healthy lifestyle takes time. It's all about time exercising, learning how to exercise, and eating right. Following me here? This all helps us to live better and longer. Investing time and effort in growing spiritually and emotionally helps us live more balanced, fruitful, and happy lives. It also, more importantly, prepares us for times of trouble, trauma, and trials. Remember the airplane emergency drill? The same thought process can be applied to life itself.

Preparing spiritually and emotionally, ahead of time, before the difficulties come (and they will), is essential. How can you handle a situation if you are not prepared? If you don't have the information or the skills, how can you respond appropriately to an emergency, a tragedy, or just a difficult decision or situation? The answer for me was obvious, only I took way too long to get it and apply that concept to my own life.

If you prepare, you will be able to "**respond**" rather than "**react**." The difference between those two concepts is huge. When your doctor says you are having a "reaction" to medication, it's always bad news and he's going to stop that med and change to another treatment plan. If the doctor says you are "responding" to medication, that's good news and it means you're probably going to get better.

The same analogy can be applied to life in general. If you invest time and effort in growing spiritually and emotionally, building healthy relationships with spouse, family, and friends, you will "respond" better than if you ignore the obvious. Not preparing means a long, "hard row to hoe." Life throws a lot of difficulties at us, always has and always will. I promise that investing in spiritual and emotional growth will go a long way to being able to successfully handle whatever life throws at you.

Don't Delegate the Important Stuff

In my own experience, delegating the emotional and spiritual growth of myself and my family to my spouse did not prepare me at all for the sudden and tragic issues that left me widowed with two daughters, one with special needs. My "reaction" left me with long-lasting emotional issues and a fractured relationship with my daughter. It caused me to not have friends or seek groups to help me sort things out. I sought distraction from the issues and my feelings in "shopping therapy" (that's another story).

If I had been prepared for this life-changing event by investing in spiritual growth, a closer personal relationship with God, and building a community of believers around me, I would have "responded" a whole lot better with better outcomes for me and my family. But I didn't prepare myself and "I did it my way." I did it the way I had always done it, facing life without letting anyone else in. I grew up in the "Me Generation" of the 1960s and the mantra was "if it feels good, do it." The result was that I believed that I could figure everything out without listening to sage advice or wise counsel.

Well, we have to change the engines while in the flight we call life. Life does not pause or allow a time out to go back and prepare for what life has thrown at us. We can't call "time out"

> **Well, we have to change the engines while in the flight we call life. Life does not pause or allow a time out to go back and prepare for what life has thrown at us.**

and land to fix what's broken. We have to do a little bit every day, take it in small bites with the long view that life is a series of short races. Life is not one long race, because that viewpoint caused me to get discouraged and tell myself "what's the point?" If life was such a long race, why bother? I recall the old motivational example of viewing the whole beach and seeing a huge obstacle, or honing in on a grain of sand and dealing with the issue one grain at a time.

Small Bites

Or, even the old question, "How do you eat an elephant?" Answer: "One bite at a time." Each day we can take one bite or pick up one grain of sand. But in the long view, taking one bite or lifting up one grain of sand at a time will ultimately lead to big accomplishments in the future.

Want a happy life, the abundant life? Then pick up a small piece every day, take a small bite every day, and that is how you do it.

How do we Manage Distractions?

First of all, let's get rid of the obviously really bad distractions like addictions. These are the no-brainers. We've been told since childhood that there are some things to never get involved with. Kinda like don't touch a hot stove, or don't stick a pin in the electrical plug (my younger brother tried both).

Alcohol and Drugs

These are obvious distractions that everyone should be able to identify and deal with; sadly, some don't or can't without help.

Alcohol and drugs cause more destruction, tragedy, sadness, and failure than anything else in our lives combined. That's my opinion, based on having lived a long time, studied history (ask my family), and had significant personal experience with drugs, alcohol, and foolish behavior. Wisdom is formed from the accumulated experiences of others, personal experiences, and plain common sense, and my wise advice is to stop drugging at all and using alcohol to excess! Any addiction to drugs or alcohol is deadly. Please get professional help, now! You cannot do it by yourself.

Addictions are Tragic

I have a huge amount of empathy for those who are addicted to drugs or alcohol. Being enslaved to a chemical that compels behaviors that destroy your physical body, your emotional and rational mind, and the personal, family, and societal structure around you is truly an evil work. These demons of alcohol and drug addictions have been working and destroying lives and cultures since the beginning of time, and there is no end in sight.

Plants of our planet were created originally to provide for our good, either directly as food or indirectly as the natural beauty of creation to be admired and wondered at. Man, in his sinful state and with Satan's help, has taken the beauty of creation to use it for evil purposes. If the process of creating alcoholic beverages had never been discovered, used and perfected, would we ever miss it? My thought is no. We never would have missed beverages that would accentuate our sinful nature. They don't hydrate our bodies, satisfy our thirst, or contribute to a healthy lifestyle in any way. You don't have to be a scientist to understand simple facts.

As one who, in the distant past, has partaken of all kinds of alcoholic beverages, a number of herbal and pharmaceutical creations – and to excess, I might add – I can emphatically say that these things have not contributed to anything positive in my life except one, and that is the clear understanding of don't do it, don't start, don't continue, but do stop and stop immediately.

Use, continued and prolonged use, keeps a person trapped in an altered state that was never intended for us by our Creator. God created everything in existence for our good. Satan assisted a sinful mankind to turn what was intended for good into something that is used for evil. The only "altered state" I want is to have God or one of His angels speaking directly to me! It's happened once and I can say it changed my life at that time and place.

Meddling?

This is a difficult topic to write about. Many will see it as meddling, others as hypocritical, and some as just nonsense. However, if a few see it as helpful in seeing the truth that alcohol is frequently destructive and disruptive, then it's worth the criticism.

Drug use is an even more dangerous behavior to become involved with. I have known many people who would never drink but have misused drugs to sleep, relieve pain, feel happy, feel down, build muscles, hide from troubles, or just avoid real life. I grew to understand as I got older that the effect of drug misuse was not a singular event. It affects many around the user, and that's as sad a sight as watching one person destroy their life, let alone many others.

All you have to do is read the headlines any day from any source to see the issues we face with drug use. It is destroying cities, neighborhoods, families, schools, you name it. It can destroy a nation, an entire generation, and the enemy is happy because we are doing all the work. Satan is laughing because he doesn't have to lift a finger because we are doing the heavy lifting to kill and destroy ourselves.

Sex, Lust, and Pornography

Gotta get healthy on this one. Pornography, adultery, lusting with the eyes can be as destructive individually and collectively as alcohol or drug addiction. Many times it's all wrapped up together in one big ball of garbage, one addiction fueling another.

There is so much in today's world that is based on sex issues, fulfilling individual desires, and expressing one's self through sex. It is one of the most powerful emotions that God created in us. God meant it to be for our good, but Satan uses it for his purposes because he knows the power it has over humans.

Previously, I said that men (not to exclude women) must avoid isolation because that is where our minds begin to fantasize to mitigate our feelings of loneliness, and many times these feelings morph into desires to possess, dominate, and control women, in the case of men. Men are not alone in this. Women are increasingly drawn to pornography, even many owning porn production companies.

At my worst point, when I was living almost totally in my own head, I was resorting to viewing pornography to alleviate my feelings of loneliness and detachment brought on by isolation – all my own doing.

It Begins at an Early Age

It eventually figured prominently in the dissolution of my marriage of twenty years. The time I spent viewing pornography contributed to diminishing the efforts (and the lack thereof) spent on building or maintaining the relationship with my spouse. My desires for relationship evaporated as I became obsessed with two-dimensional false images of women.

My attraction to pornography began at age 10 when I stumbled on my grandfather's collection of *Playboy* magazines in his nightstand. It was amplified in my late teens when I got to college. There I was in a situation of no accountability for me and magazines at the convenience store were plentiful and easy to purchase.

This obsession, which I now know as a stronghold or idol, caused me to begin to view women I would see in public as objects to be possessed in some way. This discussion may be too much for some, but it reflects a critical area of life in today's world. I confess that, as I have been writing this book, I gradually found myself downplaying what I was writing to minimize my own issues and began to preach rather than being real, transparent, and genuine. These are three attributes I have pledged myself to develop and demonstrate every day in every way.

Envy: This one sucks us all in.

This is a trap that all of us can and will be sucked into at one time or another. We are conditioned to the desire for more, better, the latest possessions or lifestyle, by influences being bombarded from everywhere all the time.

> "The world is not driven by Greed, it's driven by Envy."
> (Charlie Munger, Vice Chairman of Berkshire Hathaway)

I set out to address greed and avarice but ran across this quote that hits the nail on the head. Billionaire investor Charlie Munger said he's never cared about comparing his riches to the money of others. Rather, he says his "motivation in accumulating wealth has always been about securing independence, the freedom to do what he wishes in business and in life — and he wishes more people would follow his example."

The 98-year-old (he has passed as of this writing), who had amassed a fortune that *Forbes* estimated at $2.2 billion, added that it's easy and common for people to become envious. No matter how much some people have, someone else will always have more, he noted.

It's a sentiment that Munger has expressed in the past, and one he's previously attributed to his longtime friend and investment partner, Warren Buffett. But Munger seems confident that he's overcome the tendency himself. "I have conquered envy in my own life. I don't envy anybody," Munger said. "I don't give a damn what someone else has. But other people are driven crazy by it."

Money, success, house, cars, possessions, lifestyle – we deserve some, but you must be very certain none of these things are a product of envy or greed in your life. How big a home do you need? How expensive a car do you need? How many, how much, do you need of anything to feel better? Are you buying things, acquiring more to satisfy you, or to have more than your neighbors?

> How big a home do you need? How expensive a car do you need? How many, how much, do you need of anything to feel better? Are you buying things, acquiring more to satisfy you, or to have more than your neighbors?

When things become more important to you than your spiritual health, your physical health, and relationships with your family, friends, and above all God, they have become idols. Idols are something you worship above all other things.

Our Children

The generations behind us are a legacy. God says He loves everyone and everyone is worth saving but not all will heed the invitation. He will send an army to find us, the shepherd will leave the flock to find the one lost sheep.

You are Responsible *To* the Following Generation but You are not Responsible *For* Them. Children who leave the church versus children who stay in the church when they leave home are not necessarily reflective of the job the parents have done. Regardless, most parents did the best they could while they were raising their kids.

Three Key Insights about Young Adults Around the World

Shortly before the COVID-19 pandemic, Barna Group published *The Connected Generation*, a first-of-its-kind study, created in partnership with World Vision. The global study offered an unprecedented look at the faith and well-being of young adults—in this case, 18–35-year-olds—in 25 countries.

Loneliness, Isolation and Anxiety… plagued young adults even before the pandemic. In 2019, just one in three 18–35-year-old respondents shared with Barna that they often felt deeply cared for by those around them (33%), or that someone believed in them (32%). Meanwhile, nearly one in four (23%) acknowledged encountering feelings of loneliness and isolation.

When respondents had an opportunity to provide a portrait of their emotions to Barna, the image was one of a generation gripped by worry. Anxiety about important decisions was widespread in the connected generation (40%), as well as uncertainty about the future (40%), a fear of failure (40%) and a pressure to be successful (36%).

"Our generation has a huge amount of difficulty because we're trying to get meaning from a smaller, select group of things," explains Jefferson Bethke (author, speaker and podcaster). "Realistically, the promise the world is giving us, in a consumerist mentality, is an individual dream or promise.

"The meaning or connection you get from neighborhood, from family, from living in one location your whole life, from religion ... all these things that really anchor you are starting to go away, one by one."

Despite Recognizing a Leadership Crisis, Young Adults Aren't Always Ready to Step Up

For good reason, young adults perceive deep, wide, systemic problems facing the world's future. As of 2019, four out of five 18–35-year-olds affirmed—and nearly half strongly affirmed—that "society is facing a crisis of leadership because there are not enough good leaders right now" (82%). This was one of the most widely endorsed statements in the entire global survey, which suggests its significance to this generation. In addition, one-third believed that "what it takes to be an effective leader seems to be changing."

Barna asked young adults in what areas of their life they exercise some level of leadership. Nearly half said they were a leader in their family, and one-third felt like a leader in their workplace or elsewhere, such as a church or government. For this specific study, Barna grouped the latter into a category called "leaders outside the home," who are half of all respondents (51%); one in five was a "family-only leader" (19%), meaning they selected family as their only sphere of leadership. Three in 10 young adults did not consider themselves to be a leader, at that time (8%) or ever (22%); we referred to them as "non-leaders," accordingly. (Barna)

If children can only understand that they have so many gifts, so much talent, so much to offer the world, they would not be depressed, hopeless...

A fisherman from the Philippines leaving his heart on the stage, a 10-year-old singing their heart out, a music teacher from the south coast of the UK, hula hoops on fire – there is no limit to the creative talent of the human spirit. I am constantly amazed at the best of what the human race demonstrates of the creative power of God.

Read the News, Really

Read the news, whether in the newspaper, Internet, Tiktok, Twitter, phone, it doesn't matter. Read it only once or twice, maybe, just to get the point. Take note or measure your emotional reaction to what you are reading or viewing. Are you reacting or responding to the subject or content? Now here's the rub. Are you transferring that reaction or response to the people involved in the story? I think it's nearly impossible for us to not transfer the emotional feelings to the people. Those people qualify as your neighbors as in "love your neighbor as yourself."

We have to be able to separate the issue from the people. You can disagree or disavow the actions, positions, or statements from the people who are involved. Can you say to yourself, "I don't like or agree with what you are saying or doing, but I love you"?

If you can successfully do that, you have taken a big step to being able to genuinely love the person or people but not the actions. That is what we are called to do by Jesus when He said what He said in Matthew 22:37-40.

"All of me, why not take all of me. Can't you see I'm no good without you?"

These lyrics from the song written in 1931, most famously sung by Billie Holiday in 1941, can be applied to all of us and the way we need each other, all of creation needs all of us. It's a perfect metaphor for God's commandment to "love your neighbor as yourself."

The Last Idol (for some)

Distractions are the modern day version and epitome of idols and idolatry that have been around since Genesis of the Old Testament. Let me say quickly that idols and idolatry are what caused God to flood the earth and start over with Noah and his crew. So, let's not soft-soap or whitewash today's versions of idolatry and idols we benignly label as "just distractions." Idolatry is distraction and it causes death. Ouch! Touches a nerve, doesn't it? Anything that interferes with our main purpose – God's two most important commandments of love God, and love your neighbor as yourself – is simply bad news. Loving God involves prayer.

Idols and idolatry are the distractions we face every day in our walk with God. For me, the last idol is definitely lust of the eyes. I look at, and have always looked at, women for their beauty, and at my worst I would mentally possess them by imagining them beside me, with me, and part of me. Sounds kinda sick, doesn't it? I believe it is, but it is what drives the desire to view pornography. I'm not a psychologist or counselor of any sort, but I speak from personal experience of someone who has, as far back as I can remember, lusted with my eyes, which led me to viewing pornography, destroying relationships and eventually a marriage.

> **Loving God involves prayer.**

Idols, Idols, and More Idols

There are so many distractions in today's world that you cannot name them all. I will name a few, maybe some of the biggest, some of the most common, and some of the most egregious.

Let me explain my take on the distraction or idol that afflicts so many men, and now many women: pornography. I do not claim to be an expert on pornography, and I'm not a psychologist or trained counselor, but I have had long experience with the topic as it has affected my life in tragic ways. I am here to tell you my experience as a survivor of this dastardly distraction and idol.

Random Thoughts (but not really random)

I imagine a game of Texas Hold'em. I have just pushed "all-in."

God is in charge of my life and Jesus is my agent.

Loving your neighbor may mean not dwelling on what you disagree about but finding what you can agree upon. Ask questions until you find those things.

What is the faith, and therefore the eternity of your children and your grandchildren? You live today for them. God is faithful down to your children's children. *"But from everlasting to everlasting the Lord's love is with those who fear him, and his righteousness with their children's children, with those who keep his covenant and remember to obey his precepts."* (Psalm 103:17-18 NIV)

Chapter Nine
THE PRIME DIRECTIVE

The Plan, God's Prime Directive (any *Star Trek* fans?)

"My Way," sung by Frank Sinatra, along with the '60s vibe of my teenage years, namely "if it feels good, do it," gave me the idea that I could figure everything out about and throughout life by myself. I didn't need anybody's help, guidance, advice, or to benefit from their experience. I would learn by doing, by failing, and getting up to try again. *"What, me?"* (Alfred E. Newman, *Mad Magazine*)

Don't Have to Wait for Wisdom Until You Get Old!

Wisdom doesn't come along on its own at a certain age or in a certain place. You have to seek it, find it, and embrace it.

Some may think that it's ok for an old guy to come to "ah-ha's" and realizations or revelations at his "advanced" age, but it's too hard or outside of norms for younger folks to consider. *Look at all we younger people, including believers, have to struggle with in this world. You old people are on your way out, but we're still here (in the world) and we don't have time to think and reflect.*

My prayer every morning before my feet hit the floor is, "Lord, help me today to become the man you created me to be." Become the man God created you to be: the father, husband, son, brother, friend, employee, employer, and servant. Become the woman God created you to be: the wife, mother, daughter, sister, friend, employee, employer, a servant of others. Start every day with this being the first thought in your mind and I guarantee it will be a better day for all.

Faced with the prospect of a life I wasn't expecting or prepared for, I came to the realization that I would have to change everything about the way I lived each day if I were to successfully navigate the rest of my life. At that point it was fairly selfish motivation, but it started me on the right path.

Begin every day with prayer and reading. This simple two-step program changed my life, from here on out, after a lifetime of ignoring the Source of wisdom, knowledge, and purpose. I knew this simple fact 45 years ago, to put it in perspective. So, why didn't I start doing it back then? That is the reason for this book. As my daddy said, "Too soon old, too late smart." Well, the point is and I'm here to tell you that it's never too late: never too late to start, to grow, to impact and lead generations behind you. It's never too late to change a life, your life, your loved one's

> **It's never too late: never too late to start, to grow, to impact and lead generations behind you. It's never too late to change a life, your life, your loved one's lives, and everyone around you.**

lives, and everyone around you. "You can do it" is a line out of a movie or tv show or whatever, but it is a universal truth. You <u>can</u> do it.

Love Others as Yourself

> *"Live wisely among those who are not believers and make the most out of every opportunity."* (Colossians 4:5 NLT)

How do we do that? It seems like a really difficult deal. We live in a world that is not a Christian world. There is much evil in the world. Evil is everywhere you look. There can be no argument on that.

New believers are undoubtedly blown away by this idea that the world is evil and we can't change it. We have to live in it and still follow Jesus. The fact is that God has work for us to do, just as the new believers in the first century after the crucifixion knew they had to build the church. We have the same command, build the church, and that job will not be finished until Jesus returns.

Living Godly Lives in a Pagan Society

How do we do that? Every day it seems like a monumental task. I know I had trouble just getting up each morning feeling like the day was all about struggle. I got tired just thinking about it. But the good, no, *great* news is that we have a plan given to us in the Bible.

> *Dear friends, I urge you, as foreigners and exiles, to abstain from sinful desires, which wage war against your soul.*
>
> *Live such good lives among the pagans that, though they accuse you of doing wrong, they may*

see your good deeds and glorify God on the day he visits us. Submit yourselves for the Lord's sake to every human authority: whether to the emperor, as the supreme authority, or to governors, who are sent by him to punish those who do wrong and to commend those who do right. For it is God's will that by doing good you should silence the ignorant talk of foolish people. Live as free people, but do not use your freedom as a coverup for evil; live as God's slaves.

Show proper respect to everyone, love the family of believers, fear God, honor the emperor. Slaves, in reverent fear of God submit yourselves to your masters, not only to those who are good and considerate, but also to those who are harsh. For it is commendable if someone bears up under the pain of unjust suffering because they are conscious of God. But how is it to your credit if you receive a beating for doing wrong and endure it? But if you suffer for doing good and you endure it, this is commendable before God.

To this you were called, because Christ suffered for you, leaving you an example that you should follow in his steps.

"He committed no sin, and no deceit was found in his mouth." When they hurled their insults at him, he did not retaliate; when he suffered, he made no threats. Instead, he entrusted himself to him who judges justly. "He himself bore our sins" in his body on the cross, so that we might die to sins and live for righteousness; "by his wounds you have been healed." For "you were like sheep going astray," but now you have returned to the Shepherd and Overseer of your souls. (1 Peter 2:11-25)

Never Say "I Don't Care..."

...to anyone. This phrase is one of the most **disrespectful** and **dismissive** phrases in the English language, and I am certain the sentiment exists in almost every language in the world. I used to say those words to my parents, my spouse, and my children, and I am now mortified with the memory. I used it when I ran out of reasonable arguments or responses to whatever someone was saying to me. I used it when I just wanted the conversation to end, for the person to go away or just shut up. Ugh, there's another ugly term you should never, ever use again. There are more phrases and words like that that I may identify later.

How to Love Your Neighbors (and who are they?)

How do we love our neighbors who:

Attack our spiritual and moral beliefs;

Provide our children in school with pornographic and evil knowledge;

Seek our exclusion and cancel us from society;

Actively endanger our children;

Aggressively move to destroy our nation;

Just try to rewrite our history in a spirit of unforgiveness and hatefulness?

    I don't know, except to prayerfully ask God to show me how to love my "enemies." My enemies are my neighbors who could become my brothers and sisters in Christ. So, God, help me, show me, and lead me to understand how to love everyone, as You have commanded.

> *"When they have really learned to love their neighbors as themselves, they will be allowed to love themselves as their neighbors."* (C.S. Lewis)

A very real struggle confronted me when I came to writing about neighbors, as in "love your neighbors" as in Jesus' commandments in Matthew 22. I began writing this book with that as a main topic I felt very strongly about. It revealed itself as one of my biggest strongholds and has taken me a long time to navigate through.

In the course of writing about who God thinks our neighbors are, I felt compelled to make a list of everyone in the world that made me anxious, fearful, angry, uncomfortable, or who I thought less of, looked down upon, or I thought hated me, wanted to kill me, or I just plain didn't like for some reason. It was very revealing and, unfortunately, it was very long (disappointingly so).

Who are our neighbors, and how do we reach the point of loving them, no matter what?

I thought I was making remarkable progress toward loving everybody. After writing the list, I had to think again. All I can say now is that I am a work in progress; God knows it and grants me the grace to continue working on it, with His help.

Here's the list I made of those I had trouble loving: it includes "neighbors" who scare me, create anxiety, or who

I just don't like the way they think. Make your own list, it can be revealing and make you think long and hard, in case you didn't know what to pray about.

I emphasize that this is the list I have made after *beginning* the process of changing the way I think about everything, and in the process rewiring my brain with the help of professionals, counselors, study, and much prayer. I will tell you that the list is shorter now, but it's a work, rather I'm a work, still "in progress."

My parents raised me to treat everyone with dignity and respect and I never behaved with bias or prejudice toward anyone that I remember.

But as I grew up, all these confused thoughts began to swirl around in my head for all these years until circumstances forced me to decide to change. When I found myself in those circumstances, I truly believed my life depended on changing everything about how I thought about everything at that moment in my life.

Political: All political thought processes not in line with mine: that includes liberals, Democrats, Libertarians, Communists, Socialists, supporters of Vladimir Putin, the old Soviet system, the communist governments in China and North Korea, the Iranian government, anyone opposed to free speech, those who desire to censor free speech, and those who take gross advantage of free speech – oh, and I can't forget the Southern Poverty Law Center, a left-wing socialist bunch of anarchists, and Antifa and other anarchists.

Also eleven varieties of 'isms: anti-capitalism, anarchism, medievalism, nationalism, socialism, communism, fascism, populism, racism, environmentalism, and subjectivism.

Social: Illegal immigrants, KKK, people who believe they are victims and blame others for their self-induced issues, environmental activists, anti-fossil fuel activists, climate change activists.

General: People who buy electric cars before it's possible or practical to recycle the batteries, manufacturers who won't be responsible for recycling everything they manufacture, educators who promote their personal social ideologies to students.

Religious: Atheists, all non-evangelical Christians who don't believe specifically what I believe, anyone who hates God or doesn't believe there is a god, followers of other religions such as Muslims, Buddhists, Mormons, Christian Science, Scientologists to name a few, and men from anywhere who believe they can dominate, control, and abuse women and children.

Criminals: Pedophiles, murderers, enslavers, and wife abusers, anyone who cheats or steals from the less fortunate, veterans, and the elderly.

Personal: People who lack common sense (according to my definition), people with no mechanical or technical skill or awareness, people who can't change a flat tire, people who don't have the oil in their car changed every 3,000 to 5,000 miles, or don't know which way to turn a screw to tighten it, and last but not least, people who don't have a flashlight in their car (and phones don't count).

This is a quick list of my neighbors that Jesus commands us (me) to love and who I have had difficulty loving as He commanded. But I'm much better now.

My first thought when I read the news, heard about an event, or the thought just popped into my head, was that those on my list of offenders I should send into exile somewhere. A one-way ticket on a plane or boat to somewhere would do it. I just wanted to get them out of my life. The thought here is that I didn't have a problem, they did. I don't have a problem with them having their views and beliefs, but they had the problem of not being "right."

> **Once I accepted responsibility for being the one with the problem, I could start to get better.**

Guess what? You already guessed it, I am the one with the problem. Once I accepted responsibility for being the one with the problem, I could start to get better.

I played a game in my head called "In my perfect world." In my perfect world you wouldn't be here and it's very lonely.

I believe I played that head game most of my life. It was an easy way to slot or put people into categories where I could not think about them temporarily. I was using this process to deal with people to not have to think about them as a neighbor, a brother or sister, who God was expecting me to help, even love. It was a simple head game that made me feel better for a moment. It certainly didn't solve any problems, not mine, not theirs, not anybody's. It was very dismissive of people and I now regret it. What a colossal waste of time. But, and that's a big but, I still struggle some with this issue. I think it's not hard to grasp the concept of loving God, but it's very difficult for most of us to love our neighbors. At least many of us don't do a very good job of it.

I realize that thinking like this throughout history has led to some of the greatest examples of man's inhumanity to man. I don't even want to list them, but you know what I'm talking about.

Is it so Important to be Right? What if Being Right Every Day Means You'll be Wrong on the Last Day?

Is it important to be "right"? Or is it, as Jesus says, imperative to love our neighbors without reservation, and not to even think about being "right"? If we could only just get past our desire to be right.

I have come to the conclusion that I am the one who has the problem and "they" don't, because there is no problem – just a different way of thinking, and I am not the judge of what's right and wrong for others, certainly not non-believers. Believers and I at least start on the same page, even if some of us veer off from time to time. God will sort us all out one day.

When I decide to hate, dislike, disapprove, segregate, feel anxious, fearful, hateful, resentful, desirous of retribution, correction, punishment, exile or even elimination, I have the problem.

Love does not discriminate for any reason. Love is unconditional. When there are conditions for love, there is no love, pure and simple.

God loves all His creations without reservation. He knows we will sin but does not love us any the less. He doesn't like the way we treat each other, and when we don't love Him or his creations. We even don't like ourselves many times, or most of us much of the time. You know it's true.

If we have a list like I do, and we all do or did to some extent, we are eliminating I'm guessing a major portion of all the human beings on this planet from our being able to disciple them. If, for example, you have the "other" political party on your list and engage in angry, ugly rhetoric opposing them and their views, you have eliminated at least fifty percent of the people in America Jesus commanded us to love….as ourselves, much less persuade them a different viewpoint has merit and deserves their support.

It's Not About Being Right; It's About Loving the Other Person, Pure and Simple

Talk about second chances, l watch AGT, The Voice, BGT and the X-Factor for inspiration and motivation. Watching those shows I see all kinds of people trying to sing, do magic, perform some astounding feat, laying themselves out there for thousands of people they don't know to show them they can do something they have always dreamed of doing. They take risks, baring their souls, exposing themselves to failure, ridicule, ignominy, but standing on that stage and delivering a performance at great personal risk, sometimes triumphing, sometimes not, but always succeeding.

I believe the definition of success is trying, attempting the difficult, the seemingly insurmountable and sometimes winning but always succeeding. The motto of one of the most famous special operations military organizations on earth is the British Special Air Service (SAS). Their motto is "Who dares wins." This motto is sewn on the uniform sleeves of every trooper as part of their insignia, a winged dagger on a black field. The meaning, to me, although I didn't ask, is the effort to succeed is everything and almost always leads to accomplishment of the mission assigned. It doesn't guarantee that everyone comes home alive, but you can't succeed if you don't first dare to win. You can't win a race if you never start. You can't win a friend if you don't reach out.

The more I watch what goes on in the world the more I open up to differences, the differences in people. It takes so many, many kinds, types of people to make up this human race, this collection of God's creations making up the body of Christ. I am humbled and thankful. When we raise our consciousness above the pedestrian thoughts we humans get caught up in, we can see the heights to which God has created us to ascend.

Can what we do make other people forget about their problems, their travails, their struggles, their valleys, and think about life, about climbing their mountains and living an abundant life?

Whether you can sing a song, perform magic, fix a car, paint a picture, build a house, grow a crop, raise a child, or absolutely whatever, you are a magical creation to be celebrated, respected, honored, and loved.

It is the outpouring of emotions that energizes me watching the talent shows. I am in awe of the magnificence of God's creations and the power of His creative might. You may be a one-legged dancer from South Africa, an eleven-year-old ventriloquist from New Jersey, or anybody else who dares to try. Just try.

Volunteer....to Love Your Neighbors....Better

> *"'You must love the LORD your God with all your heart, all your soul, and all your mind.' This is the first and greatest commandment. A second is equally important: 'Love your neighbor as yourself.' The entire law and all the demands of the prophets are based on these two commandments."*(Matthew 22:37-40 NLT)

The most important commandment is to love the Lord our God. How do we manage that as the most important thing in our lives? Hint: Prayer is the answer. Prayer is talking to God, being in relationship with God, praising God, beseeching God, interceding with God, and thanking God.

How much time in our day do we spend with God? Is it an after-thought? Is it only when we are in trouble or desperate need? Is it when someone we know is in need? Or, do we tell God we love Him for no other reason than we, well, just love Him for loving us? Do we thank God for anything on a regular basis, as in daily? If the most important commandment is love God, is prayer your most important activity of the day?

> **How much time in our day do we spend with God? Is it an after-thought? Is it only when we are in trouble or desperate need?**

I know, that's a lot of questions but most are rhetorical. Yes, prayer should be the most important activity and thought every day for every believer, every professing Christian. But is it? If you believe and desire that your every step should be within God's will and design for your life, then why are we not starting everything with prayer?

We can read all there is to read, listen to every sermon there is or has been, but nothing can replace a personal and direct communication with the Creator Who is the entire reason we are believers.

I think that, with few exceptions, out of all the believers that have ever existed, most of us do not pray and commune with God every day and on a regular basis. I am going to go further and say that we should be in constant communication with God through prayer every day all day.

Now, I am not condemning or judging anyone, although you may think it sounds like I am. I am not. I am saying that we should, but knowing we won't, I am saying that we must try, we must have God in the forefront of our minds as we navigate our lives each day and through every circumstance.

This is all coming from someone who never gave God much of a thought most of his life and has arrived at a point near the end of the road and has had the bright light of wisdom go off in his head, realizing how wrong he has been. How different life could have been for everyone around him and his own self if he had only recognized sooner, had listened sooner, and been wise enough sooner – to just do it sooner.

Ah, well, "Too soon old, too late smart," as Daddy used to say.

Neighbors: Who Are They?

And then the second, but equally important, commandment is to love your neighbor as yourself. We all know the first part of that, but we often ignore the second, as in "as yourself."

Who are our neighbors? Most will think of our neighborhoods, where we live, or where we work, family, friends, or even where we worship. Let's take a look at what God says in the New Testament, Acts to be specific.

I'm going to jump through this passage to emphasize the key statements, but nothing is taken out of context.

In Acts chapter 10, beginning in verse 26, we read:

> *But Peter made him get up. "Stand up," he said, "I am only a man myself." While talking with him, Peter went inside and found a large gathering of people. He said to them: "You are well aware that it is against our law for a Jew to associate with or visit a Gentile. But God has shown me that I should not call anyone impure or unclean.*

Moving ahead:

> *"So I sent for you immediately, and it was good of you to come. Now we are all here in the presence of God to listen to everything the Lord has commanded you to tell us." Then Peter began to speak: "I now realize how true it is that God does not show favoritism but accepts from every nation the one who fears him and does what is right.*

Moving quickly:

> "All the prophets testify about him that everyone who believes in him receives forgiveness of sins through his name." While Peter was still speaking these words, the Holy Spirit came on all who heard the message. The circumcised believers who had come with Peter were astonished that the gift of the Holy Spirit had been poured out even on Gentiles.
>
> For they heard them speaking in tongues and praising God. Then Peter said, "Surely no one can stand in the way of their being baptized with water. They have received the Holy Spirit just as we have." (v. 48) So he ordered that they be baptized in the name of Jesus Christ. Then they asked Peter to stay with them for a few days.

That was long, but I included it because it answers the question of who are our neighbors. The Bible, New and Old Testaments, has many more references about who our neighbors are and who we are to tell the Good News to and accept into the body of Christ. I give only one of many examples and am hopeful it got your attention and will encourage you to study the Word and look around you to find more.

…as yourself.

All Christians will agree with the "love God and your neighbors" part, but forget the "as yourself" part. If we did, we wouldn't need psychiatrists, psychologists, and counselors to the extent we do now. How many drugs are prescribed for psychiatric or psychological issues that would not be necessary if we could grasp the enormity of two words in God's most important commandments? I stick my neck out and say far too many.

Our attempt to win the culture wars is a recipe for defeat in the battle to win souls for the Kingdom of God.

Chapter Ten

THE PROMISE OF THE ABUNDANT LIFE

"Evangelism is just one beggar telling another beggar where to find the bread."(D.Thambyrajah Niles)

One of my pastors said this to me many years ago and I thought I understood it then. But I really did not. I thought it applied to just him. It really applies to all who follow Jesus.

I'll say it again: my goal is to show and tell others where to find the bread, what to watch out for on the journey, and about the fantastic outcome that can be yours if you choose.

The ultimate goal is to live the abundant life every day. It is not just how we will live in eternity. It is a here and now thing. I grew up with the understanding that accepting Jesus as Lord and Savior, living the Christian life now and having eternal life in Heaven, was something I gained when I died. Boy, howdy, was I wrong! But it ruled my life for way too long. That view led me to "short-arm" life at every step. I lost, my family lost, and everyone around me lost.

You can stop losing and start winning right now.

The Value Proposition

> You can stop losing and start winning right now.

A value proposition in marketing is a concise statement of the benefits that a company is delivering to customers who buy its products or services. It serves as a declaration of intent, both inside the company and in the marketplace.

The term *value proposition* is believed to have first appeared in a McKinsey & Co. industry research paper in 1988, which defined it as "a clear, simple statement of the benefits, both tangible and intangible, that the company will provide, along with the approximate price it will charge each customer segment for those benefits."

- A company's value proposition tells a customer the number one reason why a product or service is best suited for that particular customer.
- A value proposition should be communicated to customers directly, either via the company's website or other marketing or advertising materials.
- Value propositions can follow different formats, as long as they are "on brand," unique, and specific to the company in question.
- A successful value proposition should be persuasive and help turn a prospect into a paying customer.

What is *your* value proposition? Why should people do business with you, buy your products or services? This could be the most important statement you can make in business and in life itself. It functioned in first century and it is valid today.

How does a business concept relate to a person's life, your life or mine? The concept of a value proposition is borrowed from a book written by Todd Duncan, who I had the privilege of working with. Todd is speaker, trainer, and author, and one of his foundational principles in business is the value proposition concept. It works in business, any business, and it is very applicable to anyone's personal life.

A value proposition in a personal life is simply wrapped up in a purpose, a set of values and personal integrity. Why are you here? What is your purpose? What do you believe are your guiding principles and how do you relate to others? It sounds so simple, but we all have so much trouble defining ourselves in these terms and living them out every day with everyone with whom we interact.

On the other hand, it's not really that complicated. "Do unto others as you would have them do unto you." Sounds familiar doesn't it? Having said all this, it gets around to how do you plan to live each day? That decision will determine the quality and effectiveness of your life and the lives of others around you. If you get it right, or close to right, and are always improving, you can live the life God has promised to us, the abundant life, a Life Without Lack (Dallas Willard), a life in the Kingdom of God here and now, on earth as it is in heaven. Yea!

What Do You Have to Gain?

Eternal life is forever and abundant life now, not just later. What is abundant life?

> *"Blessed is the one who perseveres under trial because, having stood the test, that person will receive the crown of life that the Lord has promised to those who love him."* (James 1:12 NIV)

> Jesus said, *"The thief comes only to steal and kill and destroy. I came that they may have life and have it abundantly."* (John 10:10 ESV)

Unlike a thief, the Lord Jesus does not come for selfish reasons. He comes to give, not to get. He comes that people may have life in Him that is meaningful, purposeful, joyful, and eternal. We receive this abundant life the moment we accept Him as our Savior.

Abundant life is eternal life, a life that begins the moment we come to Christ and receive Him as Savior, and goes on throughout all eternity. The biblical definition of life — specifically eternal life — is provided by Jesus Himself: *"Now this is eternal life: that they may know you, the only true God, and Jesus Christ, whom you have sent"* (John 17:3). This definition makes no mention of length of days, health, prosperity, family, or occupation. As a matter of fact, the only thing it does mention is knowledge of God, which is the key to a truly abundant life.

What is the abundant life? First, abundance is spiritual abundance, not material. In fact, God is not overly concerned with the physical circumstances of our lives. He assures us that we need not worry about what we will eat or wear

(Matthew 6:25-32; Philippians 4:19). Physical blessings may or may not be part of a God-centered life; neither our wealth nor our poverty is a sure indication of our standing with God. Solomon had all the material blessings available to a man, yet found it all to be meaningless (Ecclesiastes 5:10-15). Paul, on the other hand, was content in whatever physical circumstances he found himself (Philippians 4:11-12).

Second, eternal life, the life a Christian is truly concerned with, is not determined by duration but by a relationship with God. This is why, once we are converted and receive the gift of the Holy Spirit, we are said to have eternal life already (1 John 5:11-13), though not, of course, in its fullness. Length of life on earth is not synonymous with abundant life.

Although we are naturally desirous of material things, as Christians our perspective on life must be revolutionized (Romans 12:2). Just as we become new creations when we come to Christ (2 Corinthians 5:17), so must our understanding of "abundance" be transformed. True abundant life consists of an abundance of love, joy, peace, and the rest of the fruits of the Spirit (Galatians 5:22-23), not an abundance of "stuff." It consists of life that is eternal, and, therefore, our interest is in the eternal, not the temporal. Paul admonishes us, "Set your minds on things above, not on earthly things. For you died, and your life is now hidden with Christ in God" (Colossians 3:2-3).

> **The abundant life here in the present is a personal relationship with God through Jesus Christ. It is a focus on the eternal, not the material; the future, not the present.**

The abundant life here in the present is a personal relationship with God through Jesus Christ. It is a focus on the eternal, not the material; the future, not the present; and in a new purpose in fulfilling God's commandments through Jesus of love your God and love your neighbor as yourself.

Simple? Yes, but hard to focus on with all the distractions of this world, a world that is dominated by Satan, but only until Jesus returns.

Guys, men, I'm addressing this one to you. Just sitting in the garage doesn't make you a car. Church is the same way. You can't just sit in church on Sundays and fulfill your God-given role in your family, your church body and community. Get involved in actively becoming a follower and lover of Jesus. This is something you can't pick up from association with a church or a godly wife. Listen carefully, because I speak from hard, personal experience.

> *"Prayer is an important part of the abundant life."* (John Eldridge)

Do not fool yourself about prayer and your role as the leader in your family. You are the leader, but I am not saying or implying that your wife does not play a vital role. She does, and, if you are not fulfilling your role as leader, it creates a vacuum of leadership. Anyone can tell you that in a vacuum of leadership, someone will step up and assume the role. I can tell you that the wife will not like it, was not designed to be the leader, the warrior in the family, and all kinds of issues will arise from this situation.

I speak directly from a place of not stepping up to be the leader in my relationships with my spouses. I abdicated the function of praying, volunteering, cultivating relationships, and, to a large extent, decision making. Just ask your wife to pick a restaurant when you are going out. I never would choose and my excuse was I just wanted her to be happy with the choice. Even if you experience having your first, second, and third choices rejected, make the choices and just work it out. Choose, lead, it's ok to have a strong opinion. And it's ok to compromise, but make the choice!

Spiritual "Parents." This phrase I heard in a Sunday sermon that got me thinking about the people in my life that I knew were praying for me. At the time I thought, "That's nice," and shrugged it off. Now I can see how the Body of Christ was caring for me and loving me with prayers, just as we are commanded to do in Scripture. One person in particular I will single out because she prayed for me over many years, my Aunt Arlene. Aunt Arlene was my dad's younger sister (one of five sisters) who passed away at 98 years old just a couple of years ago. Even when she was bedridden in later years, she would call me on my birthday, ask how I was, and tell me that she prayed for me every day. This got easier after cell phones came along, but, again, it was something I shrugged off then but now I see God was at work on me through the prayers of an angel, my angel, Aunt Arlene.

My "Prayer Parents" include: Jim Lewis, Zig Ziglar, John Stinebaugh, Paul Basden, Suzan Ziglar Witmeyer, among others.

Choices, Actions, and Rewiring Your Brain

The choices you make determine the outcomes and the consequences, either good or bad, for your life and of those around you. Every little choice of action, or just the thought that preceded the action, is within your ability and power to control it. It helps if you are surrounded by people who will pour good stuff into you, but good outcomes are not limited to those who grow up in a good situation. You can overcome a bad situation, but it helps if you have people who will pour the good into you along the way.

Conversely, you can grow up surrounded by a good situation but ignore all the factors you are blessed with, and make bad decisions along the way that lead to poor outcomes and unpleasant consequences.

So, what it boils down to is make good choices and your brain becomes wired physically to choose well, expect good to come, and enjoy the benefits of the abundant life. You can also make bad choices and your brain becomes physically changed or wired to take a bad path in life. Bad choices, and decisions that come from bad choices, reinforce each other and the tendency is to continue on that path.

However, bad choices, bad decisions, and a bad path in life are not carved in stone. You can change the outcome and the path you may be on if you will recognize and admit the facts and the truth. You will still experience the consequences, but you can begin to rewire the brain and learn to make better choices that lead to better actions and build a better life.

Everything you think and do affects more than just you. Choices and actions affect everyone around you and those who come into contact with you. It's not about just you. Your family, friends, co-workers, and many, many more who you do not know or may never know are affected by your choices and actions.

This is the truth. It is reality. Reality is not a video game, a reality show, a movie, or just fantasies. Reality is who you are, who you want to be, and your goals. You can achieve the best if you are committed to changing what you think, the choices you make, and the actions you take. Then your path in life and everyone you affect around you will take you towards the abundant life.

Change Requires Effort

What does it take to rewire your brain? You have to change the input. Input is what you read, watch, listen to, or experience. GIGO, garbage in garbage out. Everything you experience is all loaded with distractions. Examine all those inputs and you will recognize good, poor, and outright bad distractions. You can eliminate the bad and the poor distractions. You can modify and control the good ones. Then you can replace what you have eliminated or modified with better. Make sense?

You only have so much time in your life and room in your conscious thoughts on any given day, so why not improve, replace, and create good, powerful, and beneficial thoughts which lead to good choices which lead to good actions and, finally, a life on the path of an abundant life?

Pick Up Your Cross and Follow Jesus

You no longer need to worry about the distractions of money, cars, homes, clothes, schools, and all the trappings of material life. God knows what you need. Be content with what you have and all you need will be provided. Find your purpose in God's will. All you need you have already to get started, and what you lack will be given. Being content within God's will for your life is known as the abundant life. A life without worry was what I sought. I found that the less I worried and the more I trusted God, the less I worried. Cute but true.

> **God knows what you need. Be content with what you have and all you need will be provided. Find your purpose in God's will.**

> *"Kindness is the language which the deaf can hear and the blind can see."* (Mark Twain)

Sleep when you are old, except when you are old you can't sleep.

Be aware and alert for "Divine Appointments"

Every day is an opportunity to share your love of God and Jesus by exemplifying how your faith has made you feel, behave, and love. Smile, share, connect – but don't preach. Treat every encounter as a divine appointment, meant to be and engineered by God for good and the building of His Kingdom here on earth. You have no idea what's going on in the life of each person you meet every day until you open up to connect with them on a personal level. Ask questions, listen intently, and be genuine.

Live Intentionally, Not by Default

Instead of wandering aimlessly through each day and eventually through life, be purposeful and intentional in what you are doing, with whom you are doing it, and aiming for the results you desire.

As my story has shown, you can't waste a life wandering through it and hope to accomplish meaningful goals and leave a legacy for future generations. Wandering without intentionality is a complete waste of time and energy. It creates anxiety, fear, and failure.

What is Your Purpose and Are You Abiding?

There is no other feeling in life that compares to abiding, being in fellowship with God.

Are you living your purpose or God's purpose? That is the question you must answer.

I Learn From Every Encounter

Just had a talk with my neighbor and I went upstairs to my apartment and began to write as a result of our conversation. It stimulated my thoughts. Everyone you talk to will teach a lesson.

I pray that this book changes at least one person's life as it has changed my life writing it. I pray one thing I have written in this book may mean something to someone, no matter how small or insignificant it seems now. Just one thing for one person in one moment can mean a life is changed and a new future is created that otherwise would not exist. Then again, if hundreds of thousands of lives are changed, that would be ok too.

Let Me Insert Here: Above and Beyond

Every person who identifies as an American, regardless of religious beliefs, political persuasion, gender, color of skin, family situation, must answer a call to serve the common good of this country.

Make this world, this country, state, city, neighborhood, church, family, a better place by choosing to become a better person, inside and out. Become a better parent, spouse, friend, brother, sister, citizen – you get the picture. A better person can make a difference everywhere, every day. Without the clichés, you can't toss off the responsibility to someone else. You can't delegate *better* to someone else and expect *better* to just happen.

You can't become a better person inside by pointing a finger outwardly to illuminate the faults in other people. When you point your finger at someone else, look at your hand. There are four fingers pointing back at you, the ultimate source of your discontent. Life's rules and instruction manual are really simple in theory, but can be difficult in practice.

Intentional Living Leads to Abundant Living and the Converse is Living by Default

If you keep living governed by your sinful nature, but expect a different outcome, that is the very definition of INSANITY.

I have been going through the process of learning to die to self for the past four years. I have learned that to die to self is a daily process and it's not easy to start. It becomes easier if you realize a journey of a thousand leagues is really only one step at a time.

Tear Down Your Idols and Remove the Distractions That are Keeping You from Living an Abundant Life

Your life in today's world is inundated by idols or distractions that prevent, obscure, and hide from view the most important point of life: Love God with all your heart, with all your mind, and with all your soul, and then love your neighbor as yourself. How do you love God, your neighbors, and yourself? Relationships are the foundation and key to loving God, your neighbor, and yourself.

Distractions can become idols and will rule your life, determine how you live, act, and love. Think about it; distractions becoming idols and having control of everything in your life. Scary. It is easier to remove or modify a distraction than it is to remove what has become an idol or addiction, something you think you cannot live without.

Nothing Happens Overnight, right away, or on our timeline. All happens in God's time if you are a believer. If you are not a believer yet, then you won't necessarily understand why, how, and when things in your life happen. But it all happens in God's time, according to His plan for your life. And I assure you, God knows you, loves you, and has a plan for your life, even before you believe, or even if you never believe.

> But it all happens in God's time, according to His plan for your life.

Lose Control

I used to get very annoyed at the thought that someone else, not me, had a plan for my life and was working to make my life conform to the plan. I was never happy, always troubled, until I let go and let God. It happened to be long after I believed in God and accepted that Jesus was my Lord and Savior that I let go of the control I thought I had and let God guide my steps. Then I found the peace I had always sought but never found. I am so comfortable living within God's will for my life, staying in my lane, within the curbs of life, that nothing can compare now to then in my life.

"Drift"

Daily staying within the will of God means walking with God, but what happens in real, everyday life is we "drift" and stray from our walk with God. One tool to maintain daily focus is the Full Focus Planner (Michael Hyatt). Granted, it is not a digital tool like everything else today, but often, if not most of the time, writing something down is far superior to trying to just remember a task, a goal, a purpose, a mission, or a guiding principle. I know that if I try to remember five things I want to accomplish tomorrow, I will forget one or two of them if I do not write it down or at least enter it into a note-taking app on my phone or in the notebook I usually carry.

Writing my story and this book caused me to re-examine my life, how I got to this point, why I made the decisions I made, and how I could have changed course without changing where I have ended up. However, I would not change where I am today because I'm right where God wants me. The free will God gave Adam and Eve in the Garden of Eden allowed me to make some poor decisions, some bad ones, some good decisions and few awesome decisions. God knew what He was doing when He deemed it a good idea to create free will. The reason is simple.

True love cannot be forced; it, by definition, can only be true if it is given freely. It is not the power of making choices that are neither determined by natural causality nor predestined by fate or divine will. God knew what He was doing before He did it. True love can only be given if it is completely the decision of the giver. God did not want love given because He said so or because it was a rule or command.

Now, the reason I've said all that is to urge you to write your story. It never has to be published, except in your own mind. But the process has the power to reveal yourself to you. Sounds redundant but it's not. It will show you how and why you became you, why you act and think the way you do. Now, it's important that what you write down is true, honest, and sincere. That may not come out immediately, but as you persevere and continue to write, you will begin to strip away the lies you have told yourself and others. You see, we lie to ourselves because we are the most susceptible to believing our own lies that end up controlling our behavior.

All that to say, the lies we have told ourselves along with the lies others have told us, and they do, forms the basis of how we view the world and our neighbors in it. All of our false beliefs, prejudices and biases are just that, lies. God did not create us with inborn bias and prejudice. We start learning from the moment we come into the world what the world is teaching us. Later, when we become aware, we learn from family one set of biases and prejudices, then school teaches us another set, and finally, the world at large teaches us another set.

And We End Up with Who We Are Today. Again, simple, right?

But, we have the manual that can bring us back to the person, the unique individual, the soul that God created. It's called God's Word. I have read it in fits and starts all my life. As a boy I didn't understand most of it, only that it was important, but not specifically for me. As I grew older, I came to believe it was very important, embodied wisdom, but again it wasn't for me specifically. Then, when I first became a believer I tried to read it and understand what it meant for me, but I still didn't get it. But when God finally got my full attention, I began to immerse myself in the Word as if my life depended on it – and it does.

It took a while to understand true meaning, nuances, context and applications, but I persevered and it all started to make sense. So, when I woke up at 5 am that Saturday morning in May two years ago, I began the journey. This book is a call to you to follow, because it's been the most exciting and fulfilling journey of my life – and I pray it will be for you, too.

Chapter Eleven

K.I.S.S.

Hallelujah! We're there…the goal, the object, and the purpose of this story, my story, your story and the beginning of a new story. I'm doing my best with what I've got to tell the story and I am prayerful that I've done an adequate job in the process. We are at the "what's next."

I grew up in post-World War II America and I'm not exaggerating when I say our society was conservative if not outright ridiculous. Then came the '60s with the counterculture revolution, the "if it feels good, do it," vibe, and the civil rights movement. That merged into the anti-war movement, and I don't know what was going on in the '80s.

Somewhere in the 2020s, concurrent with the COVID-19 virus epidemic, the "Woke" culture movement surfaced like a bad hangover. It seemed to surface out of nowhere, but in retrospect, I believe it came from decades of revisionist education in our schools and universities. Just my opinion at this point, but the "bad hangover" comment above may refer to the affluence and permissiveness in our society this century.

Warning: Personal opinion coming. We have not had real leadership in America since Ronald Reagan was our president. Give that some thought.

"Woke" Culture

Today's "Woke" culture would have canceled most of the greatest creations, inventions, and revelations of mankind as it is canceling much of our culture today. "Wokeness" surely would have tried to cancel Jesus! Jesus stepped on a lot of toes and specifically commented on everything that ruled the culture of His time and our consciousness today, and everything he did say is totally relevant today and will be tomorrow.

Everything God had to say to us is said somewhere in the 66 books of the Bible. The focus of Jesus' ministry and the New Covenant or New Testament is there for us to read. Jesus focused only on the heart and soul of the person, not anything on the exterior, not the behavior or sin of the person, nothing but the heart and soul.

The soul is what God creates. Then He provides the physical vehicle for the soul but only for the lifetime of the human body. The body has an expiration date, the same as everything on earth that is perishable. Then the soul moves on to one of two places but the body is no more. The soul remains as the existential expression of existence. It is the real person; the rest is just window dressing. Deal with the soul and you deal with everything else. When you change the soul, you change behavior and, ultimately, the outcomes in the physical world. Make sense?

I know, I may be making all this too simple for some, but I'm a bottom-line kind of person and when it (whatever we are talking about) becomes too complicated, I lose focus, my eyes glaze over and I tune out. So, you can make it simple or complicated but the results, the destination, remain the same. Keep that in mind.

Keep it Simple

A well-known author and speaker once remarked that all of his books and presentations were written at a level everyone could understand.

> *"Most management books spend some time looking at behavioral scientists' view of motivation, and this can be so technical it is difficult to understand. My approach will seem to some an oversimplification, but as I have often said, some of the greatest truths in life are the simplest. For that reason, I generally speak and write at the seventh grade, third-month level. I've also found that if I keep it at this level, even college professors will be able to keep up with me. But as my good friend Dr. Steve Franklin, who was a college professor at Emory University in Atlanta, Georgia, at the time he gave me the preceding line says, 'The great truths in life are the simple ones. You don't need three moving parts or four syllables for something to be significant.'"* (Zig Ziglar, author and speaker)

In the same vein, when Jesus spoke, He was very clear and searingly to the point with His words, even though at the time and even now, some people don't "get it." In other words, Jesus spoke in concepts that were radically different than His audiences at that time were used to. They couldn't make the mental adjustments necessary to understand that Jesus was presenting the dawn of a different concept, a new covenant.

The Bible was originally written in three languages: Hebrew, Aramaic, and Koine Greek. It has been translated into 704 languages as of 2020, the New Testament into 1550 languages, and parts of the Bible into 1660 additional languages. But in all that, the message of God comes through crystal clearly. God created us, loves us, and desires us all, everyone, to love Him, each other, and ourselves.

In order for us to do that He gave us the Bible as His story so that we can come to know Him. It's the instruction manual to know how to live and love each other and God. Then, and only then, will we be able to live the abundant life here on earth, share it with others, then join God in heaven for eternity.

I said I like to keep it simple. This is simply stated so everyone can understand it. It follows the K.I.S.S. principle and everyone can understand it, no matter where they live, what language they speak, what their nationality is, or simply anything.

My First Thought of the Day

I don't remember where I heard this, but I have been saying this prayer almost every morning before my feet hit the floor. It starts my day on a high note. Most of the time it means another great day but, of course, some days end up short of great, maybe just good.

> "Lord, help me today to become the man You created me to be."

It's short, simple, and to the point. I really do begin every day with this prayer. Occasionally, I realize I'm running late and throw the covers back and hit the ground running, or my phone has notified me of a text and I grab it to see who needs help or to reschedule a meeting, but I always pray my prayer later. This prayer truly does start me off in a positive frame of mind and spirit.

> "Lord, help me today to become the man You created me to be."

"Lord" is my acknowledgement that He is my King, my confidant, my friend, and my everything. I am reminding myself that God will lead me today and His will be done here on earth as it is in heaven.

"Help" is my cry for help from the only Source in the universe that can help me, will always hear me, and will answer my cry.

"Me" is personalizing my call to God. It's really saying "hi" to a friend, restating our personal relationship, and reaffirming that everything today starts with me and God connecting with each other.

"Become" is acknowledging that I am on a journey that will not end until I am home with Him. I am becoming the man He designed me to be and today will be one more step in that direction.

"The man" reminds me that I am a man, I'm not God, and not to forget it.

"<u>You</u>" reminds me that I know my Creator and I give Him all the glory and praise He deserves.

"<u>Created</u>" reminds me that I am special, created by God, and in no other way did I come to exist.

"<u>Me</u>" again personalizes my prayer, reminds me that He created me and each person who ever lived.

And finally, "<u>To be</u>" is the topping on the cake. It reminds me that God has a plan specifically for my life, if I will only listen to Him and follow the plan because I love and trust Him with my life. It reminds me that life is a journey and I need only to focus on the next step.

Change Your Mindset

"God, I need your help today, as I do every day, and today is not an exception. I want to become the man You desire me to be and not to follow my own guesswork, shoot-from-the-hip plan, which has led me to disaster in the past. I am going to respond to Your leading and not react to what the world throws at me.

"You created me; I am not a chance occurrence in the universe, only just one of billions of all the people who have ever lived. And You have a plan for my life. This is not a fairytale I have dreamed up on my own, a wish or a "goal" I have created because I read a self-help book, or even just the best I can do when hit with the world's idea of what I should do.

"I aspire only to become the man You have designed and created me to be. Someone who will fit into the plan You have designed for all believers to work together as the body of Your church to create Your 'kingdom on earth as it is in heaven.'"

"I Love it When a Plan Comes Together." (John "Hannibal" Smith, the A Team)

The plan is created by the Master Creator, God, and it is customized just for me as are the plans for every one of His creations, if only we would acknowledge Him, accept, believe and submit our lives to Him…every day. This is the way I counter over 60 years of "doing it my way" and continue the process of rewiring my brain to undo the years of worldly programming I allowed to run my life.

You will have to change the way you approach life every day in every way if you are to overcome what the world has conditioned you for and constantly throws at you. If the first thoughts of your waking day start with a focus on the true center of the universe, the rest of your day will follow. It will be the consistent and constant reprogramming that will change your life and the lives of everyone around you.

Hey, Y'all

This call to whatever was etched into my memories as the signal that lunch or dinner was ready and to "come and get it," or the bus was leaving, and was voiced by my father-in-law, Zig Ziglar. It is so a part of the family lore that the whole family has dish towels with that phrase printed on it. *Y'all* means you all, all of you, and you need to listen up and heed the words you are hearing … or reading.

You can substitute yourself into this prayer as in: "Lord, help me today to become the….man, woman, wife, husband, son, daughter, brother, sister, friend, employee, employer, follower or leader.... You created me to be." Try inserting the word you feel led to, depending on how you feel each day. It's not a magic formula; it's a conversation starter each day with your Creator, God. It will lead you to a deeper relationship with the Holy Spirit and the teachings of Jesus.

Each day can be, and should be, a long conversation with God. He wants to hear from you. He knows your thoughts before your lips form them. Read Psalm 139:4, *"Before a word is on my tongue you, Lord, know it completely."* He knows, but wants you to verbalize it. He wants to hear your voice, your words, and you need to hear yourself voice your prayers and concerns. Hey, if you want to know more about God, read Psalm 139 in its entirety. It's a good, no, a *great* one.

Defining the Abundant Life

I realize that I am not a learned theologian, rather just a guy who has struggled to understand and obey God's commandments. So, I ask that you don't judge me too harshly if I over-simplify something. I'm just a guy who has spent a lifetime not getting it but now has had the light of understanding turned on. I am compelled to share my story with others and I hope it's enough to start or help you on your journey.

I've said it before and I'll say it again, I'm just a beggar telling other beggars where to find the bread.

Abundant living is living within God's will for your life. In John 10:10, Jesus said, *"The thief comes only to steal and kill and destroy. I came that they may have life and have it abundantly"* (ESV). Unlike a thief, the Lord Jesus does not come for selfish reasons. He comes to give, not to get. He comes that people may have life in Him that is meaningful, purposeful, joyful, and eternal. We receive access to this abundant life the moment we accept Him as our Savior.

This word "abundant" in the Greek is *perisson*, meaning "exceedingly, very highly, beyond measure, more, superfluous, a quantity so abundant as to be considerably more than what one would expect or anticipate." In short, Jesus promises us a life far better than we could ever imagine, a concept reminiscent of 1 Corinthians 2:9: *"No eye has seen, no ear has heard, no mind has conceived what God has prepared for those who love him."* The apostle Paul tells us that God is able to do exceedingly abundantly above all that we ask or think, and He does it by His power, a power that is at work within us if we belong to Him (Ephesians 3:20).

I grew up as many Christians do, believing that the abundant life is something to experience after this life, when we die and go to heaven. I never felt it was something that I could enjoy here in this life. I didn't get it until very recently. Only when I set out to rewire my brain and approach my life as a believer in totally different ways, did I come to realize that the abundant life is not a place. It is my life today, here and now, that I can enjoy when I realize my purpose that God has given me, and live this life within His will for my life.

What the Abundant Life is Not

It is not life according to what some have called the "prosperity gospel." You are not promised financial success if you believe in Jesus and send money to a ministry so they will send you a handkerchief that has been blessed or a vial of water from the Jordan River, or whatever. God is not a cosmic vending machine that will bless you with material possessions or financial success because of your actions or your works. It does not work that way and, unfortunately, many believers have been led astray by deceitful preachers with just that promise.

> **God is not a cosmic vending machine that will bless you with material possessions or financial success because of your actions or your works.**

I promise that as you change your perspective and pursue Jesus just as He pursues you, the abundant life will come closer to where you can see it and actually feel it, as I do. I can feel it, a real physical feeling, when I believe I am living within God's will for my life, when I am in close relationship to Him. It begins every day with my starting prayer asking for God's help and praising Him.

Don't Jump the Curbs

This phrase "jumping the curbs" means to me that I have taken control back from God and I'm leaning on my own wisdom (or none at all). Remember, I've admitted that going my own way, following my own "wisdom," is what led me to disaster. So, if you regard Scripture, the Gospels, and the words of God and Jesus as the "curbs" of the road of life, then you really don't want to "jump the curb." I promise, it's a bad state of affairs leading to sometimes tragic results. At some time everyone, I think, I hope, will come to the conclusion that relying only on your own "wisdom" is a fool's journey. It's hard, it's hurtful, and it's downright dumb in all cases.

You can survive the "my way" approach but you will suffer the consequences in all cases. There are consequences in going your own way, depending on your own wisdom, and there are consequences of staying within God's will for your life. One set of consequences is ultimately bad and the other, God's plan, is good, in the long run and the short run. It's all-the-time good to stay within the curbs, God's will, and so, too, for your family, loved ones, and everyone else (your neighbors) whom you influence in your life.

How much more rewarding is it to live life every day relying on the immutable wisdom of the Creator of the universe? Sometimes the wisdom I receive from God through the Holy Spirit or the teachings of Jesus are difficult to follow, hard to swallow, and don't seem to make sense to my sinful mind, but in all cases, it is the best wisdom, the right wisdom, and the only truly good wisdom that you will ever find. There is none to compare. Always consider the source of knowledge and wisdom. Some will seem okay, but consider the source, <u>always</u>.

I know many theologically sound Christians who accept knowledge and therefore wisdom from other than sound sources. Sometimes advice, reason, and wisdom appear to not conflict with Biblical teaching but the danger is subtle. The enemy is very good at making his lie seem acceptable or even better than God's Word on the subject. If we are not practicing discernment as Jesus tells us to do, we run the risk of going down a rabbit trail that leads us away from the truth and into trouble.

As an example, there is a popular personality test called Enneagram. It was developed from disputed contemporary approaches principally derived from teachings of the Bolivian psycho-spiritual teacher Oscar Ichazo in the 1950s. You can read up on it for yourself through the Internet, but the bottom line is that it is dismissed by personality assessment experts as pseudoscience and not accepted by relevant academic communities.

There are hundreds, if not thousands, of philosophies out there that sound good, may approach a level similar to Christianity, and serve to distract believers from the correct path. Believers can and must check everything against Scripture to determine its value and veracity.

Confessions of an Axxhxxe

There's a saying I started this book with. It's not old, and I have no idea where it came from except I heard it from a good friend, Bryan Flanagan. It goes like this: "All men are axxhxxxs, but some are in 'recovery.'" Well there are many times I thought I was in recovery, but, in retrospect, I definitely was not. Not that I was always bad, I did many things right, but when I was not in recovery I hurt everyone around me.

Obviously, the most important point of life, our *raison d'être*, for even existing is to love God. The next, equally important, is to love your neighbor as yourself. After that, many of us lose track. In reading Genesis, God says in chapter two, verse 18, *"It is not good for the man to be alone. I will make a helper suitable for him."*

Then, in skipping a verse, the Scripture reads, *"But for Adam no suitable helper was found. So the Lord God caused the man to fall into a deep sleep; and while he was sleeping, he took one of the man's ribs and closed up the place with flesh. Then the Lord God made a woman from the rib he had taken out of the man, and he brought her to man. The man said, 'This is now the bone of my bones and flesh of my flesh; she will be called "woman," for she was taken out of man. For this reason a man will leave his father and mother and be united to his wife, and they shall be one flesh.'*

Now, I have applied simple (remember KISS?) logic to this passage of Scripture to make a point to illuminate the main point of life: Man and woman, having been both created by God from the same bone and flesh, for this reason will leave their families and become *one flesh*. This leads me to say with confidence that the second most important commandment after loving the Lord is to "*love my neighbor as myself.*" If the woman, your wife, is your flesh, meaning if you love yourself you must, according to simple logic, love your wife as the second most important commandment instructs us. Simple, very clear, that the most important commandments of God are to love the Lord, your neighbor, and yourself – which includes your wife! Why do men too frequently forget the last part includes loving their wife?

I did forget, to my everlasting regret. I guess Tracey got tired of living with an axxhxxe. Some people get tired of living with alcoholics, drug addicts, abusers, adulterers, and some with men who are just axxhxxes and refuse to wake up and change. And repeated doses of counseling won't work if one party is resistant to help with heels dug in against anything that hopefully would change the outcome. "Some people," including myself, simply get comfortable in their (and others') misery and are resistant to change or the promise of change.

Now guys, this is where you have to stop lying to yourself, everyone else, and get it right. Your wife is your flesh and you must love her as yourself. Of course, it doesn't work if you don't love yourself and that's where you need God to come into your life. He will help you dig out of the hole you've been living in.

And I know you can, guys, because I did, albeit too late to save a marriage. I'm also talking to women who live with men like this to know that there is always a chance for change and to seize that chance because our God is a big God and can change anyone and anything when you call on Him. It helps when you both call on Him. I say this, knowing that there are some situations that will not change and when every effort has been exhausted, it may be time to "exit stage left." But first exhaust every avenue to heal and grow. Make sense?

> **If your relationship with your spouse is not right, nothing else in your life will be right.**

This is a huge step to the ultimate goal, the abundant life. If your relationship with your spouse is not right, nothing else in your life will be right. After all, we all have heard the truism, "happy wife, happy life."

Chapter Twelve

WHAT'S THE POINT OF IT ALL AND WHY YOU?

Fun, Thrills, Excitement, Purpose, Mission, the Point of it All – and Why You?

I spent most of my life not knowing my purpose or having a mission in life. I lived life "by default." I let life come at me and I just dealt with it the best I could in the moment. It was like wading into a flowing stream and just dealing with the current and anything that floated down the river as it came at me, around me, and passed downstream. I gave little thought to the future, what next, or following any plan. My ship, my family's ship, was rudderless and a leadership vacuum existed.

The universe does not accept a vacuum, whether it's people or matter. Even space, which was thought for a long time to be a vacuum, actually has matter in it. Every organization – and families are included – abhor a vacuum. The ship sinks or the organization fails. In a family, a new leader will emerge or the family will disintegrate, or both.

In my case the "both" alternative occurred. My abdication of leadership forced my wife to take charge, which she did not want to ever do. Then the inevitable happened when I retreated further into my own head and went down the rabbit hole of pornography. Pornography is no different than actual infidelity in its emotional effect on a relationship. Ask the experts, if you will, but I can attest to that fact.

Every breed of dog has a genetic disposition for a particular job. Some for hunting, others for protection, life-saving, and some we haven't figured out yet, but they all have a job built into their DNA. All of creation has a God-given job or purpose. Every human being ever created has a desire to find what their purpose, their job in life is. It is in our DNA to find purpose and that purpose is found in God. Many of us spend most of our lives confused and wandering before we find it, if we ever do. When we don't find our purpose, it's sad and tragic. Don't pass up any opportunity to find your purpose. It could be your ticket to the abundant life our Creator promised.

Don't be Distracted

I think the Old Testament (the Jewish Scriptures) documents hundreds of laws and rules that distracted from the whole point of loving God and loving your neighbor. God did tell the Jews to take God to all nations of the world and they didn't. God gave them rules, laws, and kings because they could not keep their attention on the main point of their covenant with God. Finally, God sent His Son, Jesus, to make the laws obsolete, but complete them, be a substitute and pay the sacrifice for man's sins, and create a new covenant.

Do not make the mistake of assuming you can mix old with new – Old Covenant behavior or rules with New Covenant faith and love – for your Christian walk. I am imagining God shaking His head as many Christians try to mix old with new. They become "legalistic." Jesus was very clear that He came not to abolish the old laws, but to fulfill them. That means "we're moving on up." In the Sermon on the Mount, Jesus was speaking to the Jews in the audience. Some got it and some didn't.

The Old Testament was and still is all there is for Jews who do not accept Jesus as the Messiah. They believe in the prophecies concerning a Messiah, but they don't believe it's Jesus. The New Covenant boils down to Matthew 22: 37-40, *"Jesus replied, 'You must love the Lord your God with all your heart, all your soul, and all your mind.' This is the first and greatest commandment. A second is equally important: 'Love your neighbor as yourself.' The entire Law and all the demands of the Prophets are based on these two commandments."*

Does anyone notice that Jesus edited the most important commandments as He spoke them twice in the New Testament? Mark 12:30 is where He says, *"...love the Lord your God with all your heart, with all your soul and all your <u>strength</u>."* Then in Matthew 22 Jesus says, *"...love the Lord your God with all your heart, with all your soul and with all your <u>mind</u>.."* Interesting, but a topic for another day.

"Never forget that when we are dealing with any pleasure in its healthy, normal and satisfying form, we are, in a sense, on the Enemy's ground. I know we have won many a soul through pleasure. All the same, it is His invention, not ours.

He made the pleasures: all our research so far has not enabled us to produce one. All we can do is to encourage the humans to take the pleasures which our Enemy has produced, at times, or in ways, or in degrees, which He has forbidden." (A very good reminder about how the devil can use innocent pleasures for his own good.) (C.S. Lewis)

> **"Give every day the chance to become the most beautiful day of your life."**(Mark Twain)

Stop worrying about stuff. It creates anxiety, fear, depression, and that leads to addictions and creating idols. Why worry about stuff you have no control over? You can't change yesterday, you can't foresee or change tomorrow, and all you have is today. Why not make it the best day? Because it is the only day you have.

> **Why worry about stuff you have no control over? You can't change yesterday, you can't foresee or change tomorrow, and all you have is today. Why not make it the best day?**

Community and the Body of Christ, the Church

Men, here's another important – if not vital – subject. We must seek community, relationships, and connections with other men. Not just for business or social, not about a Linkedin network of connections, you are building the next job. Community means connections with other men who are Jesus lovers. You do this by seeking community in groups, small groups, large groups, interest groups, recovery groups, but you must be connected to men who hold the same core values you do. It means groups of men you can share your innermost issues with, even if it's only a small group.

Men who are not in community with other believers are prone to become isolated, and when isolated, men will drift into habits that will only tear them down. Isolation begets depression, anxiety, and worse, sin. Buy me a cup of coffee sometime and I can tell all about the dangers and consequences of isolation, because I've lived them.

I sat in church (and left quickly) thinking I was being a good Christian. I left the heavy lifting of serious prayer to my wives (both) and, of course, which restaurant we were going to after church. All the while I was progressively "retreating into my head."

If I've said this before, please forgive me, because it is so phenomenally vital to your Christian walk, your family's health, vitality, and happiness, vital to achieving and living the abundant life. Women need community, too. I've been apprised by one of my pastors that women are also challenged about seeking community. All believers are meant to be in community. This is how God's church works. It works best when we all come together, bringing our individual and special gifts with us. The combination of our gifts is the fuel of the church.

Think about the apostles. They were a motley crew, all very different in their gifts, temperament, abilities, and their motivation. Yet, Jesus chose them precisely because of these differences. It was not a haphazard process. Jesus looked at each one of them and said "follow Me." He did not ask them if they would like to come along, or tell them that becoming a disciple would increase their following on Twitter, TikTok or Facebook. Jesus just chose them, already knowing the gifts they brought to the party, and moved on.

They all made their decisions of their own free will and followed Jesus.

You made your decision to follow Jesus and all that decision would lead to. Get it: get the point, the point of your existence, and the reason for your creation.

It does not matter what generation you are considered to be. The Greatest Generation, born 1901-1927, is almost gone already. They lived through two world wars, a great, world-wide depression, and then led America and the world to recover from the devastation.

The Silent Generation, born 1928-1945, and Baby Boomers, born 1946-1964, are the generations that lived through the "Cold War" and through great social change. Generation X is running the world now with the Millennials or Generation Y coming on. It's Generation Z whose turn it is next to run this world (I'm still hopeful), and it's going to be interesting if the past ten years are any indication.

But my point here is that "it is what it is." We can't know what will happen in the future. We can only hope we positively influence the generations that follow us. It is our purpose to use our God-given gifts to disciple those who follow us; our families, our neighbors, and that means all of our neighbors. We must pour ourselves into every one of the different generations. They all need love, leading, learning, wisdom, support, help, generosity, food, you name it. The needs are everything and everywhere.

I'm not talking about anything new. You have heard it everywhere many times. But are we doing it everywhere, for everyone? I think not. You know it and I know it. It's an everyday challenge we must meet with our love and deeds, believe and do, faith and works.

> *"As the body without the spirit is dead, so faith without deeds is dead."*(James 2:26 NIV)

The most important commandments are very simple in theory as they are presented, but harder in practice as soon as humans begin to put them into practice. Keep It Simple Silly (KISS) is my mantra. My experience as an executive in business led me to wanting the twenty thousand foot view before I got to the operational nitty gritty. But I have found that as soon as people get involved in any process, they tend to complicate things. Life is not that complicated unless you let it become so.

Remember Occam's Razor from high school science? Simply stated it is the problem-solving principle that the simplest explanation or solution is often the best or correct one. It implies that you should not automatically search for or accept the most complicated answer to a problem.

> *"Love the Lord your God with all your heart and with all your soul and with all your mind. This is the first and greatest commandment. And the second is like it: Love your neighbor as yourself."*
> (Matthew 22:37-39, NIV)

Distractions: The bad ones are obvious: alcohol, drugs, sex or lust, and envy. The seemingly not-so-bad distractions are kids, fitness, sports, television, Internet, social media, possessions, and "busyness." We can't name them all. Anything can become a distraction from the really important things in life if you allow it to become a reason to get out of bed every morning.

An idol is a distraction that becomes more important than the really important things that should be the focus of your attention in your life. When the career or a job is more important than family considerations, your career has become an idol. When driving a fancy car or SUV is more important than having balanced family finances, then you have an idol, or when doing life your way is more important than following God's plans for your life, you have set yourself up as an idol to supplant God. And there are consequences in life for having idols. Idols require sacrifices. What are you willing to sacrifice, everything? Or are you ready to rearrange your priorities, get them in the order that honors God?

Healing Your Spirit Through Prayer, Community, and Relationships

I highly recommend getting and reading John Eldredge's book, *Moving Mountains, Praying with Passion, Confidence and Authority* , (Thomas Nelson). It definitely establishes that believers are meant to be prayer warriors and pray for healing, intervention, removing obstacles, and consecration. It reminds us that Scripture tells us to pray for guidance, understanding, and revelation. Above all, the Book tells us that we should always pray with the authority of Jesus, commanding things to come under the rule of Jesus. Powerful prayer is at the fingertips of the believer and available for every situation in life.

Community is how the body of the church works. God doesn't wave His hand and make everything happen the way He wants it. God does His work through the church. We are the fruit and the vine connects us to the body. Then, of course, God is the Gardener Who trims the vine to produce more fruit or remove dead wood.

Relationships with everybody – not just believers, but neighbors too – is how we influence and change the world. Believers need the relationships with other believers to grow, heal, and flourish as disciples of Jesus. Relationships with neighbors are how we bring the good news of Jesus to a fallen world. Become good at building relationships.

I was active in a ministry while living and working in the Atlanta, Georgia, area called Men Step Up. It was conceived and developed by Kelly Talamo and it attracted a large following of men in the area. We regularly had 50 men upward to 80, even 100, attending most Fridays at 6:30 am. I loved this because it emphasized that a man's role is to lead his family and as a leader to influence those around him. The name is straightforward in its call to men to step up and fulfill their God-given role. I call on men, fathers, husbands, sons, and brothers to step up and become the man God created them to be: warriors, leaders, and protectors.

Everyone Other than Yourself is Your Neighbor

That's right, what I've been saying. Everyone other than yourself qualifies as your neighbor and who Jesus commands us to love.

"Every one, everywhere, all the time." (Bob Goff)

Discover your purpose, mission, your place in God's plans, the most important things in life, and the real reason, the point for everything: creation, this world and you. Step out, step up, and become the person, man or woman, you were created to be.

The Abundant Life

A personal, one-on-one relationship with God is the goal. Without that relationship we are just wandering generalities in this world. The abundant life is not just for you, but also everyone around you.

> Step out, step up, and become the person, man or woman, you were created to be.

Purpose and Mission and Finding Them

This is found in the last two words of the most important commandments Jesus left us with. "…Love your neighbor as yourself." The last two words are "as yourself." This is not a "throw-away" line because, make no mistake, there are no throw-away lines in Scripture. Every word, phrase, sentence, and paragraph has meaning that God intends for us to understand and act upon.

It is never too late. I'm a prime example. I'm still a work in progress.

I love you, so go find a neighbor and commit an act of unselfish love tomorrow. Pick one of the difficult neighbors out there while you're at it.

You can have everything in life you want if you will just help enough other people get what they want. (Zig Ziglar)

My two greatest regrets up to now are not giving enough people what they wanted – unconditional love, and showing them where to find the bread. I'm working on a better answer when I'm face-to-face with Jesus.

Just another beggar...

Conclusion

What Have You Got to Lose?

What if you do make changes and what if you don't? Will it really change your life if you do make changes? Will it negatively affect your life if you don't?

Maybe it will and maybe it won't. I don't know. But what I do know is that accepting and initiating changes dramatically changed my life for the much, much better. And I know many who have experienced the positive outcomes in their lives that making positive changes have made. I also know some who, in spite of others' experiences and their own experiences, have not made changes or have reverted to former habits and patterns and have had less than positive, satisfactory, or acceptable experiences. In other words, some people keep doing what they've been doing, yet expecting different results. I think they think that trying harder and longer doing life the same old way will somehow have new and better results. That's called Insanity.

Distractions

Distractions can be all-consuming and obstruct your view of the most important point of life. Every distraction can become an idol and idols can take over your life until you are living for the idols and distractions. Then you are serving the idols and filling your life with everything except what's truly important to you and everyone around you.

The really bad distractions of alcohol and drug abuse are clearly destructive, but often are hidden from view and even from the person with the addictions. Sex or lust can be as big an addiction and equally destructive. Run for help, for rescue from the only Source in the universe that can help and more importantly, rescue.

Envy

Envy, avarice and materialism can be as big a consumer of our attention and as disruptive as the aforementioned pursuits and addictions. We live in a world, a country, a society that sells envy every hour of every day. More, better, new and improved is the message relentlessly hammered into our minds from every source of communication. And more avenues into our minds are created every day, night and day.

If you are a believer, there are many pitfalls that can divert, obstruct, and complicate our focus on the important commandments of our God. We are tempted by everything in the world and in our faith. There are many denominations, preachers, and sects that have warped and distorted the Gospel. Take for instance the "prosperity gospel" and groups that mix the Old Testament rules with New Testament love.

Kids are a huge consumer of our affection, attention, time, resources, and efforts. But how can you deny them anything when they are so precious and cute when they are young? You pledge to yourself not to deny them anything, any opportunity, any good thing. But children, like all things in our lives – including ourselves – have limits. We all are accountable to many things, and time and resources are a big part of that. We must teach the truths of life to our children, bring experiences to them that equip them for life on their own, and still have time and resources for everything else we have to manage in life.

The very most important item on your list must be God. "Love God with all your heart and with all your soul and with all your mind. And the second is like it, love your neighbor as yourself." Do this and everything else will fall into place.

Here Comes the Close

This is like the old, tried and true sales closing techniques that I learned a long time ago from the master of closing the sale, Zig Ziglar. Working side by side with Zig and being in and connected to the family for the past forty-plus years has embedded this one in my mind. It is the "impending event close." I'll explain for those who are not in sales or are new to sales. The very dramatic and effective way to successfully close a sales presentation is to make the sales offer then announce that the offer is "for a limited time only," or "if you make a buying decision now rather than later (or after I talk to someone) I can add in this or that incentive."

My point is that you can wait, think, study, research, sleep on it, ask a friend, or just put a decision off into the future. That will only delay the inevitable results or prolong the agony of life as you know it now. But, making a decision to change what you are doing that isn't working or not working well will take you one step closer to the abundant life that God has promised.

Immediate Gratification

Why wait? Why not begin enjoying the benefits right now? As I sat in my one-bedroom apartment that day in May 2019, I faced the decision you may be faced with now. Do you stop telling yourself – or listening to the world tell you – lies that everything is okay now, or do you accept and admit that you have been believing untruths about your life, your purpose, and the most important reason we exist and just go with it?

I took a lifetime to reach the point where I realized I had to make a deep-down, honest decision to change the direction of my life. You don't have to wait. The decision can be made at any time, anywhere you are in life.

Just go, light the fire, and move toward the light, it's ok.

> *"You can't start a fire without a spark."* ("Dancing in the Dark," 1984 Bruce Springsteen).

I am here to tell you that the spark has a name: Jesus. I made several commitments to truly follow Jesus during my life, but until I was faced with the totality of my actions and

Conclusion

beliefs I never made the total commitment. I realized in that moment that going forward my life depended, absolutely depended, on my decision in that specific moment to follow Jesus without doubts or hesitation. I had never "gotten it." I was just playing. I was playing me and everyone else.

Light the fire; find the spark and start, today, now, one thing, one small step for you and everyone around you. Yell "fire" and just GO and I'll see you at the party.

> You must remember this
> a kiss is just a kiss, a sigh is just a sigh
> The fundamental things apply
> as time goes by…

"As Time Goes By" (sung by Dooley Wilson in the movie *Casablanca* and later recorded by Louis Armstrong, lyrics by Herman Hupfeld)

As the song goes, "the fundamental things apply as time goes by." God is <u>The</u> Fundamental Thing, and has already written the ending for our story. So relax, never be anxious, and live the life God has all along intended for us to live.

SUGGESTED READING AND RESOURCES

Irresistible – Andy Stanley

Not In It to Win It – Andy Stanley

Finding Your Place in God's Great Story – Paul Basden & Jim Johnson

Everybody Always – Bob Goff

How We Got The Bible – Greg Lanier

How to Read the Bible for All It's Worth – Gordon Fee & Douglas Stuart

The Holy Bible (NIV & NLT) – God

In His Image – Dr. Paul Brand and Phillip Yancy

Un-Distracted – Bob Goff

The Return of the God Hypothesis – Stephen C. Meyer

See You At The Top – Zig Ziglar

Live Without Lack – Dallas Willard

Living in Christ's Presence – Dallas Willard

www.ingramcontent.com/pod-product-compliance
Lightning Source LLC
Chambersburg PA
CBHW030110170426
43198CB00009B/568